FAIREY
SWORDFISH

1934–45 (all marks)

COVER CUTAWAY: Fairey Swordfish.

(John Weal/Art Tech/Aerospace Publishing)

First published in July 2014

Jim Humberstone has asserted his moral right to be identified as the author of this work.

A catalogue record for this book is available from the British Library.

ISBN 978 0 85733 362 9

Library of Congress control no. 2013955827

Published by Haynes Publishing,
Sparkford, Yeovil,
Somerset BA22 7JJ, UK.
Tel: 01963 442030 Fax: 01963 440001
Int. tel: +44 1963 442030 Int. fax: +44 1963 440001
E-mail: sales@haynes.co.uk
Website: www.haynes.co.uk

Haynes North America Inc.,
861 Lawrence Drive, Newbury Park,
California 91320, USA.

Printed in the USA by
Odcombe Press LP,
1299 Bridgestone Parkway,
La Vergne, TN 37086.

Acknowledgements

This book has been produced with the close co-operation and support of the Fly Navy Trust and the Royal Navy Historic Flight.

The author gratefully acknowledges the wholehearted support of, and help from, the following during the preparation of this book.

Commanding officers and staff of the Royal Navy Historic Flight, past and present, in particular Lt Cdr Mike Abbey, Lt Cdr Ian Sloan and Lt Cdr Chris Götke; Swordfish pilots Lt Cdr Glenn Allison, Lt Cdr Mark Jameson, Lt Cdr Simon Wilson; Katie Campbell, Display Manager, RNHF; Howard Read, Engineering Manager, RNHF; 'Tug' Wilson, 'Fraz' Frazer, Mick Jennings, Dave Clarke and Nick Bailes, maintainers and groundcrew, RNHF; also veteran Swordfish aircrew Lt Cdrs Bruce Vibert, W.A. Reeks and R. Selley; and Mr A.W. Hodgkin (ex-Blackburns).

BAE Systems, Fleet Air Arm Museum (Barbara Gilbert), Imperial War Museum, Solent Sky Museum, Rolls-Royce Bristol, Rolls-Royce Heritage Trust, Hornet Aviation, Deltair Airmotive Ltd.

Aviation photographers Richard Mallory Allnutt/Vintage Wings of Canada and Keith Wilson/SFB Photographic.

Sincere thanks go to aviation photographer Lee Howard, many of whose stunning photographs of the Swordfish and other aircraft of the Royal Navy Historic Flight grace the pages of this book.

The author and publisher gratefully acknowledge the following publications for the use of copyright material: Moffat, John, *I Sank the Bismarck* (Bantam Press, 2009); Lamb, Charles, *War in a Stringbag* (Leo Cooper, 1987); Payne, Donald, *From the Cockpit No 10: Swordfish* (Ad Hoc Publications, 2008); Brand, Stanley, *Achtung! Swordfish! Merchant Aircraft Carriers* (Propagator Press, 2005); Forty, George, *The Battle for Malta* (Ian Allan, 2003); Ott, Frank, *Air Power at Sea in the Second World War* (Society of Friends, Fleet Air Arm Museum, 2005); Sturtivant, Ray, *The Swordfish Story* (Cassell, 2000).

FAIREY SWORDFISH

1934–45 (all marks)

Owners' Workshop Manual

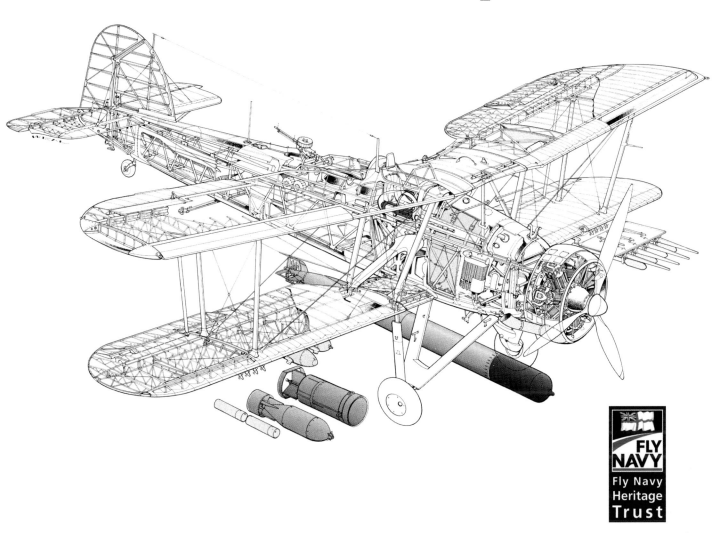

An insight into the history, development, production and role of the Second World War biplane torpedo bomber

Jim Humberstone

Contents

OPPOSITE **Fairey Swordfish Mark II, LS326, pictured on 19 July 2011.** (Lee Howard)

Introduction

The Royal Navy Historic Flight operates a flying collection of some of the rarest and most historically significant Royal Navy aircraft in the world. The Flight was established in 1972 to preserve the nation's naval aviation heritage and to serve as a living memorial to the courage and sacrifice of all those who served in the Royal Naval Air Service and Fleet Air Arm. It has three Fairey Swordfish aircraft including the oldest surviving example in the world, W5856.

LS326 against the backdrop of RNAS Yeovilton, home of the Royal Navy Historic Flight. (*Lee Howard*)

Based at RNAS Yeovilton in Somerset, the Royal Navy Historic Flight operates three historic aircraft types, each of which reflects a key period in Fleet Air Arm operations from the 1930s to the 1950s. These include the iconic Fairey Swordfish – the subject of this book – a significant national treasure embodying the very essence of the Fleet Air Arm and the wider naval ethos; the Hawker Sea Fury, the last piston-engine fighter aircraft, famously credited with shooting down an enemy jet during the Korean War; and the Hawker Sea Hawk, the only airworthy example in the world, representing the Fleet Air Arm's entry into jet-age aviation from the decks of aircraft carriers.

The aircraft display to over a million people annually at air shows and public events up and down the country, representing the Royal Navy and raising awareness of the history, technological innovation and achievements of naval aviation to wide-ranging audiences. Few people today are aware of the important part played by the Royal Naval Air Service and Fleet Air Arm in Britain's history. When they see these rare and remarkable aircraft flying they are overwhelmed by the stories of the brave young men who flew them and the heroic and daring missions they undertook.

The first aircraft to join the collection was Swordfish Mark II, LS326, which was

ABOVE Swordfish Mark II, LS326, piloted by Lt Cdr Glenn Allison over the Solent on 14 November 2010. *(Lee Howard)*

BELOW Hawker Sea Fury T20, VX281/G-RNHF, owned by Naval Aviation Limited (an off-shoot of the Fly Navy Heritage Trust) on delivery from North Weald to RNAS Yeovilton in the hands of Lt Cdr Chris Götke on 4 March 2011. The aircraft carries the markings originally worn by Sea Fury F10, TF912 ('120/VL'), of 799 Naval Air Squadron (NAS), part of the 50th Training Air Group based at Yeovilton in 1949. *(Lee Howard)*

presented to the Royal Navy in 1960 by the Westland Aircraft Company. Later additions to the collection were Hawker Sea Hawk FGA6, WV908, from RNAS Culdrose in 1982, Fairey Swordfish Mark I, W5856, as a gift from British Aerospace in 1993, and Hawker Sea Fury FB11, VR930, completely rebuilt by BAe Brough in 1997. A third Swordfish (NF389) is currently in storage and awaiting the opportunity to be rebuilt.

Additionally, the Flight operates a Sea Fury T20, G-RNHF, donated by a benefactor and maintained on the civil register. Together these magnificent aircraft are an enduring legacy of the remarkable history of naval aviation

ABOVE The 18-cylinder 2,500hp Bristol Centaurus engine in Sea Fury FB11, VR930, roars into life. *(Lee Howard)*

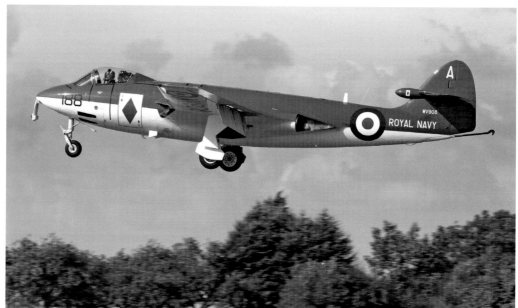

RIGHT Hawker Sea Hawk, WV908, with flaps and arrester hook down, comes in to land at RNAS Yeovilton. *(Lee Howard)*

RIGHT Swordfish Mark II, LS326, airborne with two Westland Lynx helicopters of 815 NAS over Somerset on 9 November 2010 to commemorate the 70th anniversary of the attack on the Italian battle fleet at Taranto. The Swordfish is being flown by Lt Cdr Glenn Allison. *(Lee Howard)*

ABOVE The 2012 season Royal Navy Historic Flight pilots and groundcrew with Swordfish LS326. *(Lee Howard)*

RIGHT A briefing for the pilots from the engineer. *(Lee Howard)*

providing a powerful educational link between the Royal Navy's historic past and the Fleet Air Arm's role in worldwide operations today.

The Flight is partially funded by the MoD as an operational Royal Navy unit and the commanding officer and aircrew are serving Royal Navy pilots. The maintainers and groundcrew are civilians employed under contract and considerable engineering and design support continues to be provided by the Royal Navy and by industry, principally BAE Systems, Rolls-Royce Plc and AgustaWestland. The Flight is also directly supported by the Fly Navy Heritage Trust, a registered charity that raises over £600,000 annually to supplement the operating and maintenance costs of keeping these historic and priceless aircraft flying.

RIGHT The Royal Navy Historic Flight trailer travels to air shows around the country during the display season. Display manager, Katie Campbell, is second from the left. *(Lee Howard)*

Chapter One

The Swordfish story

Perhaps the most remarkable aspect of the venerable Fairey Swordfish was its longevity. Despite its antiquated appearance it was tough and versatile and has the distinction of being one of the few aircraft that remained in operational service throughout the whole of the Second World War. It even outlasted its intended replacement, the Fairey Albacore, which was withdrawn from front-line service in 1943.

OPPOSITE The Royal Navy Historic Flight's Swordfish Mark II, LS326, pictured in 2010 on a check test flight in the Yeovilton MATZ after an 11-year absence from the display scene. The pilot is Lt Cdr Mike Abbey, the Flight's Commanding Officer at the time. *(Lee Howard)*

RIGHT Sir Richard Fairey ranked with A.V. Roe, Frederick Handley Page and the Short brothers as one of the great pioneers of British aviation. *(Copyright unknown)*

BELOW Some 800 Fairey Albacore aircraft were built to meet the needs of Air Ministry Specification 41/36. Intended as the replacement for the Swordfish it was some 20mph faster and boasted improvements like a heated cockpit enclosure and a more powerful engine with variable pitch propeller. Despite these advantages, and although it performed well, it was outshone by its predecessor and was withdrawn from front-line service before the Swordfish. *(Imperial War Museum (IWM) TR296)*

When the First World War broke out in 1914 Richard Fairey was, comparatively speaking, a newcomer to the British aviation scene. Initially qualified as an electrical engineer, like his famed contemporary A.V. Roe he had developed his enthusiasm for aviation through aero-modelling. However, he had progressed to acquire valuable aeronautical skills, eventually working as chief engineer for possibly the earliest of the country's aircraft manufacturers and the first company in the world to build production aircraft, Short Brothers on the Isle of Sheppey.

Like many of his First World War generation he was stirred to volunteer. By chance during his call-up process he met the legendary pioneer of naval aviation, Commodore Murray Sueter. Sueter was aware of the potential loss to the industry of a skilled aeronautical engineer at a time when aeroplanes were desperately needed. In his position as Director of the Air Department at the Admiralty he was able to coax Fairey away from joining the service by offering the 28-year-old a subcontract to build aircraft. This was to be arranged with the Short Brothers. Fairey would build twelve Type 827 seaplanes for the Royal Naval Air Service. Other contracts followed, including one of especial importance, that for the production of 100 1½ Strutters.

The delivery of these orders laid the foundations for one of the more successful of British aviation companies. The post-First World War period saw Fairey's emerge as one of the more individualistic and innovative aircraft manufacturers in the UK. A succession of designs was produced and went into service, principally with emphasis on the manufacturer's specialism of naval and carrier-borne machines.

During the Second World War it developed an important specialism, that of building quite large and complex carrier-borne aircraft. The Swordfish was followed by the Albacore, the Firefly and the notorious Barracuda. These developments were to culminate post-war in the dedicated variants of a state-of-the-art (but complex) anti-submarine and airborne early warning system design, the Fairey Gannet. During this period it also developed one of the most advanced experimental supersonic delta wing designs, the Fairey Delta 2.

Air-to-air guided weapons were developed by the company but Fairey's also played a part in the evolution of a very attractive light aircraft, the Tipsy, and of the production of the very successful Islander and Trislander series of small feeder airliners, as they were known. Finally, until taken over by Westland, the company was at the forefront of British helicopter development.

From the outset Sir Richard pursued his quite individual objectives and persuaded his company to venture where most other British plane makers would not go. Establishing an aviation business in Belgium as he did in the interwar period must have caused some shaking of heads, but perhaps the prime example of his unorthodoxy was the adoption in the late 1920s of an American engine, the Curtis V12, to be installed in his latest advanced biplane design. He went further and followed this by developing his own unique 24-cylinder engine which, in effect, represented an attempt to challenge the 'magic circle' of British aero-engine builders of the time – Rolls-Royce, Armstrong Siddeley, Bristol and Napier.

However, with the development by Fairey's of the TSR Swordfish in the mid-1930s, here was a company on familiar ground, confidently turning out what it knew best, developing the design of a versatile and reliable, traditionally configured naval aeroplane. It was a design which reflected decades of experience in meeting the needs of the Admiralty and its naval air arm.

Sir Richard Fairey was highly regarded throughout his later years as a member of a band that came to be called the 'knights of the skies'. Among his many accomplishments, one which he shared with another aviation 'knight' Sir T.O.M. Sopwith, was yachting. Perhaps Sir Richard's greatest achievement in this sphere was his election in 1936 to be Commodore of the prestigious Royal Yacht Squadron at Cowes.

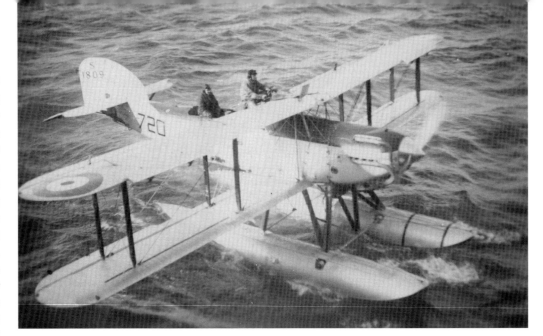

RIGHT The Fairey IIIF was designed to meet the requirements of Air Ministry Specification 19/24 as a Spotter/ Reconnaissance aircraft and served worldwide on every Royal Navy carrier. Its versatility anticipated that of its stablemate, the Swordfish, with the RAF forming bomber squadrons of the type and three even being used for radio control experiments. *(Jonathan Falconer collection)*

Evolution of the design

The interwar period of the 1920s and '30s was a difficult time for British aircraft manufacturers. The dramatic downturn in the requirement for military aircraft at the cessation of hostilities in November 1918 came as a shock to those companies who had built up substantial design and production facilities to cater for large War Office and Admiralty orders.

During the 1920s the Fairey Aviation Company, under the stewardship of the enterprising aviation pioneer Sir Richard Fairey, looked around for overseas customers to supplement the much reduced orders for the RAF and Fleet Air Arm (FAA). They found one customer in the Greek Navy and Fairey's duly supplied this service with the very successful Fairey IIIF Mark III series of three-seat reconnaissance aircraft. These aircraft, influenced by Sir Richard's enthusiasm for Curtiss airframe and engine design, were also to be used by the RAF and FAA throughout the late 1920s and early 1930s. Eventually the design spanned six different marks, the last two being named Gordon in RAF service and Seal when used by the FAA.

Role of the Swordfish

Thus the Swordfish specification, at least in part, grew out of the development of a design to replace these Greek Fairey IIIFs. However, the evolution of the design can be traced back to the summer of 1931 when

the Air Ministry, who were responsible for the procurement of both naval and military aircraft, issued Specification G.4/31. No less than nine firms submitted designs to meet its requirements, which were wide ranging and stemmed from the need to replace the Fairey Gordon and Westland Wapiti landplanes. This specification set new standards for multi-role British service machines. First choice for the RAF was a Vickers biplane design which, when modified to monoplane configuration, emerged as the Wellesley. It was eventually to prove an outstanding performer in pre-war RAF service.

It must be appreciated that the service procurement provisions at the time led to a continuous series of specification numbers which could be amalgamated or consolidated (as the mood took the Air Ministry) under other numbers and with other requirements.

At one point response to Air Ministry Specification S9/30 for a Torpedo Spotter Reconnaissance (TSR) aircraft resulted in an inline-engine machine, a joint landplane/ floatplane design. It flew in seaplane form with a large central float and wingtip stabilisers. The aircraft was powered by a Rolls-Royce Kestrel of 525hp. As installed in this S9/30 design, the engine relied on steam condensing for cooling purposes. With the Rolls-Royce power plant it looked more like a Hawker design than one by Fairey. Development of this machine proceeded in parallel with the TSR, overlapping the evolution and first flight of that design.

The TSR design that took shape as a response to these two influences evolved through the work of Marc Lobelle (Fairey's Belgian designer) aided by H.E. Chaplin. The 'Greek' design, perforce having Private Venture status (that is, with the 'PV' prefix) took to the air from Harmondsworth piloted by Chris Staniland, Fairey's CPO, on 21 March 1933.

The prototype on this first test flight was powered by an uncowled Armstrong Siddeley Panther VI twin-row 14-cylinder radial engine, giving 625hp. A short while later it was re-engined with a single-row radial, the 9-cylinder Bristol Pegasus IIM, giving slightly more horsepower and fitted with the Townend Ring. This was a close-cowled aerodynamic engine cover, evolved through the work of Dr Townend and the National Physical Laboratory at Teddington. From this point onwards the machine became known as TSR 1.

A senior naval officer played a significant role in the gestation of TSR 1. During his time as a captain working as a liaison officer at the Air Ministry, Admiral Clive Rawlings foresaw the need to add an offensive capability to the spotter- reconnaissance role already being performed by existing naval types. On his own initiative he encouraged Fairey's to pursue this objective.

The final proposals for the aircraft were submitted to the Air Ministry whose Specification S15/33 was issued in 1933. Fairey's design, the PV TSR, conformed to its requirements in all major respects.

The Torpedo Spotter Reconnaissance appellation reflected the three principal roles of the aircraft. At this stage the potential for the aircraft to perform as a bomber, either in level flight or dive-bomber configuration, would not have been fully appreciated since the circumstances that would give rise to this particular role perhaps would not then have been anticipated.

First prototype

After the first flight of the Panther-engined PV TSR which took place at Harmondsworth aerodrome to the west of London, and re-engined with the Pegasus, the prototype took to the air again on 10 July 1933. However, tests were overtaken by catastrophic failure on 11 September that year.

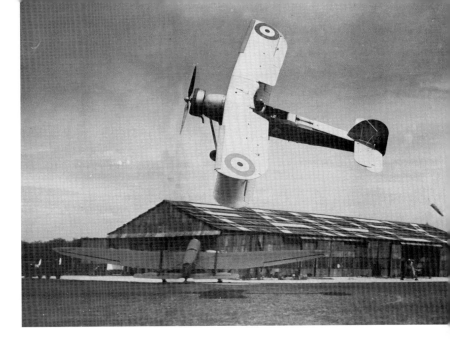

ABOVE A spectacular performance by Chris Staniland, Fairey's Chief Test Pilot, demonstrating the Swordfish prototype's superb low-speed manoeuvrability. *(Copyright unknown)*

On this occasion, having stalled, the single prototype aircraft went into an irrecoverable flat spin. Having experienced about twelve turns in this attitude and under considerable slipstream and g-forces, the test pilot, Chris

BELOW PV TSR with Pegasus IIM engine, photographed before early changes were made to the TSR prototype. These included deletion of the wheel spats and the fitting of a Townend cowling with collector exhaust ring. *(Copyright unknown)*

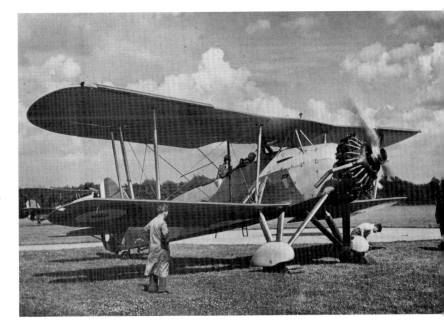

THE TSR ROLE – NAVAL RECONNAISSANCE BEFORE RADAR

The appellation Torpedo Spotter Reconnaissance (TSR) identified the fact that such a type in FAA service could perform all three roles. Prior to the introduction of seaborne radar, just being installed in His Majesty's capital ships at the outbreak of war, the TSR machines of the Royal Navy were intended to act as the principal means by which enemy naval forces could be detected at sea. It was anticipated that the war at sea, at this very early juncture, would be conducted in surface actions by major fleet units. Naval staff hardened by the confused intelligence that bedevilled Jutland were insistent that a significant role of the Navy's airborne component would be that of scouting ahead of the Fleet to provide early warning of an enemy presence. As was to be proved with the disastrous sinking of HMS *Courageous* within weeks of the outbreak of the Second World War, reconnaissance principally focussed on surface units of the enemy.

The provision of floatplanes on battleships, battle cruisers and larger cruisers proved an even more cost-effective means of meeting the reconnaissance needs of the Fleet. While aircraft, catapult and hangar might pose a weight and stability penalty, this was more than offset by the carrying of an aircraft, which had general utility, quite apart from its so-called scouting role. This capability was dramatically underlined when in the Second Battle of Narvik on 13 April 1940 the Swordfish floatplane flown off HMS *Warspite* gave a spirited performance as spotter and rounded this off by sinking the German U-boat *U64* in Rombaks Fjord.

ABOVE Swordfish K8428 from the Torpedo Trials Unit (TTU) at Gosport releases a torpedo. This photograph, taken on 22 October 1939, illustrates the low altitude required (typically 50ft) for weapon release, together with evidence of the need to achieve the optimum angle of entry of the weapon into the water. *(Copyright unknown)*

RIGHT An 818 NAS Swordfish carrying six 100lb bombs about to be launched from HMS *Ark Royal*'s starboard catapult. *(Fleet Air Arm (FAA) Museum)*

Staniland, extricated himself from the cockpit with great difficulty and took to his parachute. The prototype was totally destroyed after hitting the ground near the village of Longford, a short distance from Fairey's airfield.

TSR II second prototype

The TSR II, as the second prototype came to be known, was registered K4190 and its design reflected lessons learned from its ill-fated predecessor. This machine first flew on 17 April 1934. As a modified prototype it incorporated several changes to the original design. These included a wider chord fin and rudder, but perhaps the most important of the modifications was the lengthening of the fuselage by one bay. To compensate for this change, which affected the C of G, a four-degree backward sweep was introduced in the upper mainplanes while retaining the straight lower mainplanes to preserve their structural integrity for weapons loading.

Other important changes included the substitution of a metal, three-blade, fixed pitch propeller of Fairey Reed design for the original wooden Watts two-bladed type (a move to three metal blades later took place with both the Hurricane and Spitfire). The original wheel spats were omitted and oleo systems incorporated in the undercarriage.

Prototype trials

The prototype K4190 TSR II proceeded successfully through its manufacturer's trials with numerous (albeit minor) modifications as a result of the tests. It then proceeded for trials at the Aeroplane and Armament Experimental Establishment (A&AEE) at Martlesham Heath in Suffolk.

Generally the A&AEE reported favourably on the aircraft's behaviour, but there was concern about stall characteristics and recovery from spin. The tests were undertaken at a weight of 7,500lb, reflecting the effect of carrying a torpedo on the AUW of the aircraft.

Subsequently K4190 undertook trials on the test catapult installation at the Royal Aircraft Establishment (RAE) Farnborough, together with deck landing trials on HMS *Courageous*.

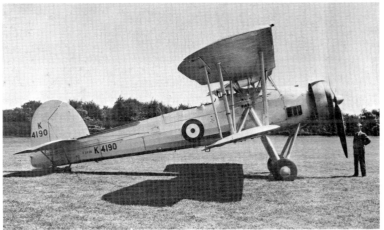

TOP A view of the prototype K4190 at an early stage in its development. Note the fitting of a two-blade propeller of simple design and the lack of sweepback to the upper main planes. *(FAA Museum)*

ABOVE K4190 in service markings revealing the effect of further changes to the prototype. *(Copyright unknown)*

BELOW K4190 in August 1937 fitted with dual control. Apart from conversion to trainer form with dual control, the much changed Swordfish prototype exhibits further modifications including heightening of the tail-wheel position, repositioning of the oil cooler and deletion of the anti-spin strakes. *(Copyright unknown)*

Then in November 1934 K4190, fitted with twin floats, made its first flight as a seaplane at Hamble. From there it moved in the New Year to the Marine Aircraft Experimental Establishment (MAEE) at Felixstowe in Suffolk for its tests on water. Eventually it arrived for its final series of tests at the Torpedo Trials Unit (TTU) at Gosport, Hampshire, in February 1935.

Once again, however, a Fairey prototype was dogged by ill luck when K4190 crashed at Gosport injuring its pilot. By this time the machine was configured in its landplane form. When rebuilt the aircraft included, among other modifications, conversion to dual control and changes to the ailerons and the oleo undercarriage elements. In its modified form K4190 served as a test aircraft for the Air Ministry's Directorate of Technical Development.

FLOATPLANE SWORDFISH

Designed from the outset for operation from land or fitted with floats, the Swordfish proved to be a most successful floatplane. The airframe was readily convertible from land to sea configuration and vice versa. The various floatplane components could be carried by Royal Navy aircraft carriers so that aircrew training could be undertaken while in harbour. For instance, in the 1930s Royal Naval Air Station (RNAS) Kalafrana on Malta would have been used by Swordfish aircrew detached from their carrier in Grand Harbour.

Perhaps the most important contribution made by Swordfish floatplanes was that of spotting for their parent warship – monitoring and correcting the fall of shot from a battleship or cruiser. This role came to the fore in three major engagements: the spotting by HMS *Warspite*'s floatplane during its Norwegian fjord action in April 1940 (as mentioned above), and similar assistance that was rendered to Royal Navy capital ships during the bombardment of the two French Fleets at Dakar and Oran in 1940.

Eventually 700 Naval Air Squadron (NAS) was formed to act as the headquarters unit for Floatplane Flights embarked aboard larger naval units such as battleships, battle cruisers and cruisers. A dozen or so Catapult Flights were included and Supermarine Walrus and Fairey Seafox aircraft were also on strength.

While the Swordfish was embarking in the larger capital ships of the Royal Navy the Fairey stablemate, the Seafox, was earning its place in naval history by spotting for the 8in cruiser HMS *Exeter*, reporting that the German pocket battleship *Graf Spee* had blown herself up off Montevideo in Uruguay.

(Significantly, an important component of the 2nd Tactical Air Force employed from D-Day 1944 onwards performed an almost identical role. Fighter squadrons of both the RAF and FAA directed ship-to-shore bombardments along the Normandy coast. Significant, also, in that these operations were directed from HMS *Daedalus* at Lee-on-the-Solent.)

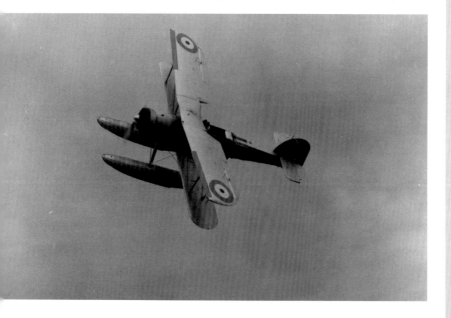

LEFT HMS *Barham* enters the Grand Harbour at Valletta in Malta. Note the 701 Catapult Flight Swordfish on X turret. *Barham* is pictured before Royal Navy battleship catapults were repositioned on deck amidships. The red, white and blue stripes on B turret were used to identify neutral warships on Neutrality Patrol during the Spanish Civil War, c.1936. *(FAA Museum)*

FAR LEFT A closer view of an X turret catapult installation with a Swordfish in situ. Retained in this position there is no doubt its presence would inhibit operation of the ship's main armament in any action. *(FAA Museum)*

LEFT A Swordfish floatplane pilot gets a piggyback ride ashore, 19 July 1941. *(FAA Museum)*

LEFT Swordfish floatplane P4202. Visible in this photograph are the torpedo sight and early camouflage marking on the aircraft's upper surfaces. *(Copyright unknown)*

ABOVE Assembly of a Swordfish Mark I nearing completion. Engine, cowling, oil and fuel tanks have been fitted by this stage. Note the early provision of the fin marking. *(Copyright unknown)*

Production stages

Eventually, by April 1935, the Swordfish had passed all its service trials. The Air Ministry then issued a contract for three pre-production aircraft. These acted as further trials machines and were subjected to a series of tests during 1935 and 1936. They underwent minor modifications including broader chord engine cowlings and the omission of anti-spin strakes. The three machines were put through a full range of trials at Martlesham Heath, Farnborough, Gosport and Felixstowe so that their behaviour as floatplanes, with torpedoes and when undergoing launches could be seen to measure up to the Air Ministry's stringent requirements.

Additional changes that had taken place during the previous two years were prompted by the low positioning of the empennage. Fairing off the lower edge of the rudder and raising the height of the tail wheel effectively overcame this problem.

An initial production order for 86 aircraft was then made and deliveries took place during the summer of 1936. These aircraft were built to Air Ministry Specification S38/34 with the Bristol Pegasus IIIM3 engine of 690hp and the aircraft were supplied with torpedo sights. Some of the early batches were involved in further service trials and as initial training aircraft, while others went into temporary storage, pending issue to operational Naval Air Stations.

The type finally entered service at Hal Far, Malta, with 825 NAS in July 1936, replacing their Fairey IIIFs. This was a little over three years after the initial flight of the first prototype and by 1938 the Swordfish had replaced all other FAA types to be its sole torpedo bomber.

The design of the Swordfish throughout the Second World War, and in its various marks, reflects responses to both the changing requirements in different theatres of operations, on land and at sea, and to the changing weapons and equipment technologies that were taking place during that time.

RIGHT Swordfish Mark I aircraft of 811 NAS overfly ships assembled for the 1937 Coronation Review at Spithead. The 8in cruiser HMS *Achilles* can be seen in the foreground, complete with her Supermarine Walrus reconnaissance amphibian on its catapult. *(FAA Museum)*

With initial deliveries from 1936 in its Mark I form, the primary role of the Swordfish was to be as a torpedo bomber. It went on to prove its worth in this role by crippling torpedo strikes against enemy battleships both at the Italian naval base at Taranto and against the German battleship *Bismarck* in the North Atlantic.

By 1943, the Mark II was rolling out of the hangars at Blackburn's. This mark reflected a new threat and a new role. The airframe was modified with strengthened metal-clad undersides to the lower mainplanes. Quadruple rocket projectile hard-points were then fitted under each wing. This enabled the Swordfish to perform as a potent rocket projectile delivery platform, thus enhancing the type's capability to serve as a critical escort component on the Arctic and Atlantic convoys.

Later that year the Mark III emerged with state-of-the-art Mark X radar, the scanner housed in a radome fairing located between the split undercarriage legs. This important development, coupled with such refinements as flame damping exhausts and the fitting of the powerful Leigh Light, came at a time when anti-U-boat patrolling increasingly presumed that such operations would be carried out at night.

The so-called Swordfish Mark IV was a Canadian version. To enable them to perform their training role in that harsh climate some were fitted with a purpose-designed enclosed canopy. There is no evidence that this change, Modification 408, resulted in the machines receiving a new mark number.

Thus it can be seen that the seeming archaic configuration of the Swordfish ensured it could accommodate a range of modernising modifications, far more readily in certain respects than its more modern counterparts. These changes fitted it for new roles, roles that were totally in accord with the changing needs of the war at sea. Summing up, it could be said it went where others could not go.

The Blackburn Swordfish

By late 1939/early 1940 with some 600 Swordfish built, Fairey's were turning their attention to deliveries of the Swordfish's intended replacement, the Albacore. The Fulmar fleet fighter was also in production by then and

design work was proceeding for other important prototypes like the Barracuda.

Faced with an overstretched plane maker, the Admiralty looked around for another manufacturer as a production source and their gaze fell on the Blackburn Company in Yorkshire. This was a firm with considerable experience of the design of naval aircraft and had been responsible for a small production run of the Swordfish's predecessor, their own Shark. The move of production to Humberside fitted in with the Ministry of Aircraft Production's (MAP) plans for dispersed production in the aircraft industry to minimise any loss of production through enemy bombing.

Blackburn's Swordfish production

With manufacture of the aircraft having passed from Fairey's factory at Hayes in west London to the Yorkshire company, production began in December 1940. Blackburn had retained its Olympia Works in Leeds despite having to give up the adjacent open space they had used as a landing ground. However, such was the nature of the new contract that the facilities at Brough were supplemented by a new factory at Sherburn in Elmet, some ten miles to the east of Leeds. The work was widely subcontracted resulting in an all too familiar dispersal of manufacturing at that time, which was based on the four main assemblies.

The first Swordfish had been delivered by the end of the year and 350 of the Mark I version were completed by the beginning of October

ABOVE The provision of a cold-weather enclosed canopy to Canadian Swordfish gave rise to the view that this constituted the Mark IV version of the aircraft. While several aircraft received this welcome unofficial modification, it did not result in a further mark number being allocated. This is Swordfish HS553.
(Jonathan Falconer collection)

RIGHT Swordfish ribs being manufactured at one of the dispersed Blackburn factories. Despite the apparent crowded conditions, Blackburn's achieved excellent Swordfish production totals in their Yorkshire factories. *(Copyright unknown)*

1941. At this point the company commenced production of the Mark II incorporating the strengthened wing. From this point onwards the pace quickened, the next 100 machines taking less than six months. The period June 1942 to February 1944 saw 900 aircraft leave the factory. At this point production was turned over to the Mark III with ASV radome. Various other minor modifications had been incorporated by this stage. The third aircrew position with its Vickers machine gun gave way to radar installation and aircraft were provided with flame

RIGHT Swordfish mainplanes being assembled in one of the Blackburn factories. In essence, the rib and spar wings shown in the photograph represent an adaptation to metal from wood of what were First World War construction techniques. *(Copyright unknown)*

damping exhausts, thus reducing their visibility during night operations.

The final batch of Swordfish numbered 320 machines and production of the type ceased with the completion of the very last aircraft, a Mark III, in mid-August 1944.

Less well known than the company's new-build endeavours was its contribution to the task of repairing Swordfish. Blackburn set up the Blackburn Repair Organisation operating at both Brough and Sherburn and dealing principally with naval aircraft.

ABOVE Tailplane assembly shop. Assembly techniques using trestles and workbenches are shown in this photograph. These arrangements reflect little change from First World War practices. (Copyright unknown)

LEFT Swordfish Mark IIIs nearing completion in the Blackburn factory at Sherburn in Elmet. ASV radomes can be seen on the right. The fuselages in the foreground are shown at their earliest stage of construction. These are juxtaposed with virtually completed aircraft that can be seen at the rear in this photograph of the Yorkshire factory. (Copyright unknown)

THE BLACKBURN MODIFICATION AND REPAIR ORGANISATIONS

These were important offshoots of the main company. The work of the former was principally taken up with modifications of newly arrived American aircraft destined for the FAA. Early in the war these had been purchased from the American manufacturer but subsequently they were Lend-Lease supplied. Martlets, Hellcats, Avengers and Corsairs all received modification after arrival in Britain.

The Repair Organisation was responsible for the modification, repair and salvage work on a range of naval aircraft. It became so important that new buildings were built at Sherburn specifically for repair work and a number of sites were requisitioned in Leeds to make up the shortfall of urgently needed floor space. Over 1,000 aircraft were returned to service under these auspices between 1940 and 1945 among which were some 130 Swordfish converted to dual control and well over 100 that were subject to electrical and other modifications.

Swordfish totals

The lion's share of Swordfish building was undertaken by the northern company. By the time production finished in 1944, Fairey's had completed 693 Mark Is and Blackburn had delivered 1,700 Marks I, II and III. This gives an approximate total of 2,400 not including 600 that were cancelled towards the war's end. With characteristic ingenuity the Navy nicknamed the North Country variety 'Blackfish' – and it is recognised among FAA Swordfish pilots that, despite a totally consistent specification, the Blackfish's origins could be distinguished through its distinctive handling from those of its original maker.

KEY EARLY AIRCRAFT

F1875 – Armstrong Siddeley Panther-engined PV TSR I (manufacturer's designation) (subsequently refitted with a Pegasus). Crashed.
K1940 – Pegasus-engined TSR II.
K5660 – Pre-production machine, to RAE and A&AEE.
K5661 – ditto – to TTU.
K5662 – ditto – to MAEE.

Swordfish in service

By 1938 the successful delivery of Swordfish from the Fairey works resulted in the equipping of all Royal Navy torpedo bomber squadrons with the aircraft. At the outbreak of war in September 1939 13 squadrons of the type formed the backbone of the Navy's torpedo strike force. By war's end a further 13 first-line squadrons had received the Swordfish. This was in addition to an RAF unit, 119 Squadron, which was equipped with ex-Royal Navy Mark IIIs and operated from Belgium on anti-submarine and anti-shipping duties in the last months of the war.

The last FAA Swordfish squadrons were stood down on 21 May 1945 with the RAF squadron following a few days later. The final flight from a carrier took place in August 1945 when a Swordfish Mark II took off from Light Fleet Carrier HMS *Ocean*. Significantly, and perhaps as a sign of respect for the old lady, it carried not just one but two flag officers on its final flight!

Other Swordfish users

As already mentioned the RAF operated the Swordfish with 119 Squadron, but it also used it on anti-aircraft co-operation work with units based at Kalafrana, Malta and Seletar, Singapore. No 202 Squadron RAF used a small number of Swordfish based on Gibraltar to patrol the Straits. A similar role was undertaken from Aden by 8 Squadron during 1940–41. Finally, the RAF gave instruction to FAA pilots between 1942 and 1945 at its 9 Advanced Flying Unit in Scotland.

The Royal Netherlands Navy also experienced the type through their contribution to the manning of the Merchant Aircraft Carrier (MAC) ships HMS *Gadila* and *Macoma*, both tanker conversions. Flights were provided by 836, 840 and 860 NAS based on shore at RNAS Maydown in Northern Ireland. A maximum of 83 aircraft were on strength at the height of their contribution to escort duties. These were embarked aboard 19 MAC ships. No 860 NAS was the last unit to receive a new Swordfish, which was delivered in June 1943.

With Canada as the first landfall on the North Atlantic convoy routes it was to be expected that the Swordfish would find a place in the history of that aviation-minded nation. Its primary role in Canada was a second-line one insofar as the Swordfish served as trainers for FAA aircrew. A RCAF Naval Air Gunners School was formed at Yarmouth, Nova Scotia, on New Year's Day 1943. At the peak of their presence there were just over 100 Swordfish aircraft in Canada. Additional second-line duties included target drogue towing and bombing practice with Swordfish on the strength of 6 Bombing and Gunnery School, Saskatoon, and 1 Wireless School at Mount Hope, Ontario.

For a brief period after the war several Swordfish (by this time transferred from RCAF to RCN charge) formed a Fleet Requirements Unit. Further use was found for the remaining aircraft by reserve units where they were employed as ground instruction airframes.

One of the more fortunate (but fortuitous) contributions made by Canadian Swordfish has been to act as a kind of repository of surplus airframes, thus ensuring the survival of a significant number of the type both as restored museum static exhibits and more spectacularly as flying examples.

ABOVE No 820 NAS was embarked on HMS *Ark Royal* during the period 1939–41. The bright peacetime markings would soon be replaced by more discreet insignia, together with upper and lower surface camouflage. These aircraft are overflying the liner *Empress of Australia*. *(FAA Museum)*

BELOW Although Swordfish were never manufactured in Canada, many were shipped across from Britain. These aircraft made a significant contribution to the Commonwealth Air Training Plan, especially those fulfilling the requirements for FAA Telegraphist/Air Gunners (TAG). Some Swordfish, like this Mark II version, survived in Canada after the end of the Second World War and were eventually returned to England for use as instructional airframes. This example is seen at RNEC Manadon in 1960. *(FAA Museum)*

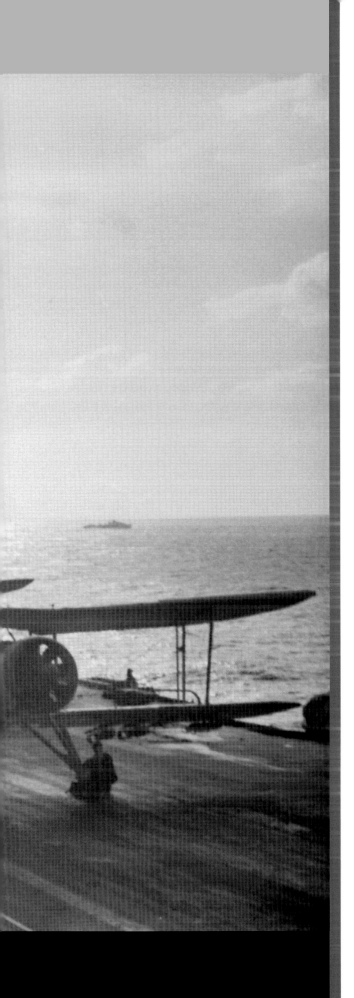

Chapter Two

Swordfish at war

The pride and esteem that the Royal Navy has in the Fairey Swordfish is easy to explain. It was a phenomenally successful combat aircraft that saw active service worldwide. Between 1939 and 1945 the Swordfish pursued the enemy, afloat and ashore, in every theatre of war, between the Atlantic and the Indian Ocean, the Equator and the Arctic Circle.

OPPOSITE Fairey Swordfish (in foreground), with Fairey Fulmars and Blackburn Skuas pictured on the deck of the aircraft carrier HMS *Ark Royal* at sea in April 1941. At this time *Ark Royal* and its Swordfish squadrons were part of Force H based at Gibraltar. This was formed to fill the gap in the western Mediterranean naval defences that came about with the loss of the French Fleet to the Allied cause, after France's capitulation. The ship astern is likely to be the battle cruiser HMS *Renown*. *(IWM A3759)*

Introduction

The date is 10 July 1940. It is just over a month since Italy declared war on Great Britain. The place, the western Mediterranean off the coast of Calabria. The Swordfish aircrew of HMS *Eagle*'s 813 NAS are not long returned from a torpedo strike on the Italian Fleet. While waiting for another sortie they are treated to the frightening spectacle of a retaliatory attack on their carrier by Italian Savoia Marchetti SM.79s. The contrast between the two aircraft could not have been more dramatic: 813 NAS equipped with a slow open-cockpit biplane, substantially fabric covered, armed with one 18in torpedo; and *Il Duce*'s airmen flying large three-engined all-metal machines at twice the speed of the Swordfish and capable of delivering up to three aerial torpedoes to the 'Stringbag's' one. If it had not sunk in before, at this point the fact would have clearly established itself in the minds of the British aviators that an immense disparity existed between their Stringbag Swordfish machines and the equivalent types that the Royal Navy would have to face, fielded by its enemies.

Swordfish into action

The course of the war was such that over time the naval action moved generally from home waters and the Atlantic to areas further afield. Significantly the initial focus of the Royal Navy and its Swordfish squadrons was to be the threat from surface raiders, as exemplified by the German Navy's pocket battleships and armed merchant raiders. By contrast the last two to three years of war saw the Stringbag play the fullest part in defeating the underwater threat posed by German U-boats, and in the very last weeks of the war in Europe the unique night-fighting qualities possessed by the Swordfish saw it come into its own.

Truly, the Stringbag was (to use another metaphor) the quintessential 'maid of all work' for both naval and military. Many were the tasks undertaken by this extraordinary and ubiquitous machine throughout the Second World War, not least its involvement in amphibious operations and support of land forces when it often operated from land bases.

However, defence of the sea lanes was, is and always will be, absolutely fundamental to the operations of the Royal Navy. 'It is upon the Navy under the good providence of God that the wealth and safety of the Kingdom do chiefly depend' say the Articles of War, 3rd Version, 1661. No words are able to sum up the Royal Navy's continuing responsibility and commitment more succinctly than these. As will be seen the Fairey Swordfish played its full part in the achievement of those objectives, from September 1939 to the war's end in August 1945.

To understand the wide range and continuity of Swordfish action it is necessary to follow the course of military and naval events as they were played out over time. First and closest to home were the Atlantic and the North Sea theatres of operation.

THE ATLANTIC
September 1939 to March 1940

The first four months of the war could be accounted a severe learning process so far as the Royal Navy was concerned. Complacency and bad tactical judgement could be said to have contributed to two major tragedies.

On the evening of 17 September 1939, less than a fortnight into hostilities, HMS *Courageous* was torpedoed by the German U-boat *U29* commanded by *Kapitänleutnant* Otto Schuhart. Some 518 men went down with the ship together with two Swordfish squadrons (811 and 812), representing some of the earliest

aircraft losses of the Second World War. HMS *Ark Royal*, pride of the carrier fleet, had already experienced a near-miss from a torpedo fired by *U39* three days earlier, a warning sign that appeared to be ignored. A further blow was struck a month later, on the night of 13–14 October, when *U47* (*Kapitänleutnant* Günther Prien) succeeded in entering the naval anchorage at Scapa Flow and torpedoed the battleship HMS *Royal Oak*.

In the aftermath, the loss at Scapa Flow was attributed to incomplete anti-submarine defences. However, in a sense the loss of *Courageous* and the incident with *Ark Royal* were more serious since they reflected a dangerous underestimation of the risks of allowing lone, weakly escorted carriers (in the case of *Courageous* by just two destroyers) to undertake anti-submarine work. In addition, both the sinkings were an early warning of the terrifying power of the torpedo, whether submersile or air-launched – a lesson the Swordfish would underline with great emphasis just over a year later.

Ark Royal with her Swordfish complement from 810, 820 and 821 NAS together with the battle cruiser HMS *Renown* formed part of Force K. This force was based on Gibraltar and was intended to make up for the now interned French warship component.

In the course of four months *Ark Royal* together with *Furious*, *Hermes* and the seaplane carrier *Albatross*, carried out wide-ranging search operations in the Atlantic, hoping to

detect German commerce raiders or their supply ships. Eight Swordfish squadrons took part. While their principal quarry eluded them the aircrews of the *Ark Royal* squadrons had some success in locating blockade runners off Spain in February 1940. Also, in mitigation of this seemingly extravagant use of scarce naval sources, it is generally accepted that awareness of a carrier at sea in any area of operation had a significant deterrent effect.

THE NORWEGIAN CAMPAIGN
April 1940
Nazi Germany invaded Norway on 9 April 1940, seeking to secure the route for its iron-ore supplies and in line with its territorial ambitions. The northernmost of the six German

ABOVE Crew abandon the aircraft carrier **HMS *Courageous*** after she suffered a fatal torpedo strike from the German U-boat, *U29* (*Kapitänleutnant* Otto Schuhart). This tragic loss occurred on 17 September 1939, only a fortnight after the outbreak of war. Some 25 Swordfish were lost together with 518 men, representing almost half the ship's company, including her captain. *(US Library of Congress)*

LEFT HMS *Ark Royal* pictured during the early months of the war launching a Swordfish. The aircraft is well airborne beyond the round-down of the flight deck and a further Swordfish waits above the ship's stern. *(FAA Museum)*

invasion groups gained the port of Narvik, while the remainder seized the major ports of Oslo, Trondheim and Bergen and other areas in the south. The Royal Navy was quickly on the scene and within a few days an Allied Expeditionary Force had been assembled and troops landed at Namsos, Andalasnes and Narvik. FAA aircraft formed part of the response of the Home Fleet.

Just two days after the invasion, Swordfish of 816 and 818 NAS embarked on HMS *Furious* attacked two German destroyers in Trondheim Fjord. Unfortunately their efforts were without success, with torpedoes grounding in the shallows.

Then from 24 April HMS *Ark Royal* and HMS *Glorious* joined in the fray. Their Swordfish squadrons lent further weight to the campaign with Swordfish from 810 and 820 NAS carrying out strikes in the Namsos area in support of Allied landings, which were intended to recapture Trondheim. The same squadrons launched a daylight attack on Vaernes airfield and on 9 May a formation of

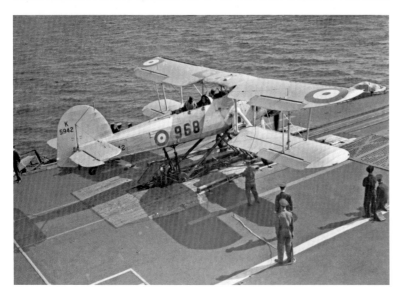

six Swordfish attacked the railway linking Norway with Sweden, damaging installations and rolling stock.

With the evacuation of Allied ground forces it was left to naval and air units to continue to harry the enemy in and off Norway.

The so-called Norwegian campaign proved to be a fruitless and costly exercise. Almost inevitably so, perhaps, bearing in mind it represented the pitting of half-trained troops and inexperienced aircrew against battle-hardened and experienced Heer and Luftwaffe personnel and their equipment.

The fighting took its toll of Allied air strength. It is believed operations in the Norway campaign resulted in the loss of nearly a dozen Swordfish, due in part to a lack of a fighter escort. Until the arrival of *Ark Royal*, strike operations had to go ahead without air cover since *Furious* had sailed from the Clyde without time to pick up her contingent of Skuas.

Finally, FAA catapult seaplanes and flying boats from the capital ships and cruisers also played a valuable part in the campaign. Six Walrus amphibian aircraft distinguished themselves, even performing the bombing role on occasion. However, a single Swordfish TSR floatplane covered itself in glory. In the course of spotting for the battleship, HMS *Warspite*'s aircraft sank the German *U64* in Rombaks Fjord. While *Warspite* and its accompanying destroyers together sank eight German destroyers, Swordfish versus U-boat was in a sense something special – a taste of things to come as later developments were to drive home.

June 1940

While Anglo-French forces were engaged in Norway during April and May 1940, RNAS Hatston-based Swordfish of a depleted 823 NAS continued their important work of mining and anti-submarine patrols.

A further opportunity to strike at the enemy arose when the German battle cruiser *Scharnhorst* was reported to be making its way back to Kiel from Trondheim. During her engagement with the aircraft carrier HMS *Glorious* and her destroyer escorts HMS *Ardent* and HMS *Acasta*, the latter in its dying moments had secured a torpedo hit on the German ship. On her way back to the north German port for repairs, *Scharnhorst* was attacked by six Swordfish from 821 and 823 NAS. Unfortunately, denied the advantage of surprise and encountering fierce AA fire from seven enemy destroyers near the ship, none of the torpedoes hit home. Losses amounted to two aircraft with four aircrew killed.

ABOVE Surviving members of 825 NAS in 1940 after attacking targets in support of retreating BEF near Dunkirk and Calais. A mixture of uniforms and ranks is evident in this photograph, including two naval ratings and two non-Royal Navy officers who were presumably attached to 825 NAS at that time. *(Copyright unknown)*

ABOVE Flying from airfields at Maleme (Crete) and Paramythia (Albania) 815 NAS flew anti-shipping and mine-laying operations in the Adriatic during March and April 1941. The squadron continued its operations from Paramythia until on 16 April German forces invaded Greece and Albania and they were forced to evacuate to Dekheila (Egypt) and then to Cyprus. L9774, 'F', in the foreground is from 814 NAS. *(FAA Museum)*

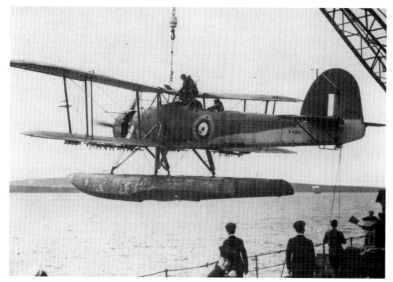

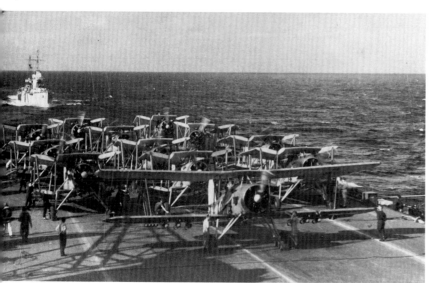

THE MEDITERRANEAN
1940–43

Vital British interests were under threat with the entry of Italy into the war in June 1940. The Mediterranean from Gibraltar through to Suez was a main artery of Empire and the opponents were a force to be reckoned with. The Italian Navy possessed a powerful modern surface fleet of battleships, cruisers and destroyers. The Royal Navy was to be stretched to its limits to maintain its influence over *Mare Nostrum* as it was called by Mussolini, *Il Duce* (particularly bearing in mind its extensive responsibilities elsewhere, at global scale).

Again the FAA was quickly on the scene. Within days of Italy's declaration of war Swordfish of 767 NAS had flown from Hyères, the French air base near Toulon in southern France, and attacked the Italian naval port of Genoa. The squadron afterwards flew on to Malta via Tunisia. As a reconstituted 830 NAS their aircraft then made a considerable contribution to the island's attacking strength, especially through taking part in night shipping strikes from the island until late 1942.

Calabria

Action was then joined at the eastern end of the Mediterranean basin. Admiral Cunningham sailed from Alexandria on 8 July with a battle fleet that included the aircraft carrier HMS *Eagle*, the battleships HMS *Warspite*, *Malaya* and *Royal Sovereign* and a cruiser squadron, as well as escorting destroyers. As a result a

CENTRE Swordfish V4367 of 701 Catapult Flight is recovered to HMS *Malaya* during October 1941. The engine is turning and the deck handling party has organised a steadying wire attached to the aircraft under its tail. *(FAA Museum)*

LEFT Swordfish from 813 and 824 NAS on the flight deck of HMS *Eagle* in 1941. With the carrier's limited flight deck width (clearly apparent in this photograph) it has been necessary to range further Swordfish, behind that about to take off, in a wings folded configuration. A destroyer, acting as the carrier's guard-ship, is stationed astern of *Eagle*. *(FAA Museum)*

strong Italian Fleet was brought to battle the next day off the Calabrian coast. During the afternoon of 9 July, while the Italian battleships were being engaged at some range by *Warspite*, Swordfish of 813 and 824 NAS flew off twice from *Eagle* to mount torpedo attacks on the Italian ships. These proved to be unsuccessful with enemy cruisers turning away under cover of smoke. Swordfish pilots distinguished themselves by beating off heavy air attacks by the Italians.

A further sortie was launched by the Swordfish of 813 NAS against the port of Augusta in Sicily in the evening of 10 July. On this occasion, whilst not encountering the main Italian units, the strike did yield hits on a tanker and the attack resulted in the sinking of a destroyer, the *Leone Pancaldo*.

During the brief lull which followed, *Eagle*'s 813 and 824 NAS aircraft were temporarily shore-based in the Western Desert. The latter squadron in particular achieved much success. During July and August 1940, two destroyers, three submarines and a depot ship were sunk in the harbours of Bomba and Tobruk.

Taranto, 11–12 November 1940

The air strike against the Italian Fleet at their Taranto base in southern Italy proved to be a textbook exercise. It represented a quick, well-planned response to what could have been a fleeting opportunity.

An attack on Taranto had been mooted as far back as the Abyssinian Crisis of 1936. During the summer of 1940 Admiral Cunningham – or 'ABC' as he was half-affectionately called – knew that carriers were becoming his trump card and that two of them

ABOVE Swordfish K8422 of HMS *Eagle* was lost on a raid on Maritza airfield in Rhodes on 4 September 1940. She is seen here with her Italian captors. Both mainplane assemblies have been removed at this stage. Clearly the downed Swordfish has attracted great interest among the Italian service personnel. *(Copyright unknown)*

ABOVE No 813 NAS initially operated Swordfish Mark Is from the aircraft carrier HMS *Illustrious* and took part in the successful raid on Taranto in November 1940. On 6 June 1941 while operating from HMS *Eagle* the squadron sank the U-boat supply ship *Elbe* and forced the tanker *Lothringen* to surrender, before returning home in October to re-equip with Swordfish and Sea Hurricane Mark Ibs. *(FAA Museum)*

RIGHT Lt Alan Downes of 830 NAS supervises the maintenance of his Swordfish. Note the overload tank in the observer's position. Utilised for the Taranto raid among other operations, it could be said that overload or auxiliary (long-range) fuel tanks played a crucial part in Swordfish successes. Apart from their somewhat precarious mounting position and occasional tendency to unship, they were regarded, in their exposed state, as one more hazard to be faced by the observer in his position in the rear cockpit. *(Copyright unknown)*

would give him much greater tactical flexibility. Thus the arrival of his state-of-the-art second carrier, the armoured HMS *Illustrious*, with its enthusiastic new carrier squadron flag officer, Rear Admiral Lyster, gave added impetus to the operation. Unlike HMS *Ark Royal* with its cruiser standard armour, *Illustrious* boasted a fully armoured hull and represented a great leap forward from the *Ark*. With armoured hangars and 3in of armour on its flight deck, the ship's design represented an effective response to the threat from the air. She also brought with her what were termed 'overload tanks', giving extra fuel capacity and enabling her complement of Swordfish to strike further from the Fleet.

The trigger for the timing of what came to be known as Operation 'Judgement' stemmed from the results of photo-reconnaissance flown to *Illustrious* on 11 November. A Malta-based RAF Maryland of 431 Flight piloted by Flt Lt Adrian Warburton had over-flown Taranto on the 10th and confirmed that five battleships and several other large warships were at anchor in the inner and outer harbours. It was believed a sixth battleship would shortly be joining the others and this was later confirmed by an RAF Sunderland.

The arrival of HMS *Illustrious* from the West Indies in the eastern Mediterranean cannot be over-emphasised. Unfortunately Cunningham's other ship was the small and ageing HMS *Eagle*. This had a limited aircraft capacity of 24 aircraft, being only two-thirds the complement of *Illustrious*.

As luck would have it both carriers had suffered problems in the lead-up to the attack, originally scheduled for Trafalgar Day

(21 October). *Eagle* had aviation fuel problems and *Illustrious* experienced a hangar fire. In the circumstances, six Swordfish were moved from *Eagle* to *Illustrious*. These made up a striking force of 21 aircraft, 3 fewer than planned due to recent ditchings; 17 of the aircraft were armed with torpedoes and 4 with flares and bombs. Four NAS participated – 813, 815, 819 and 824.

The strike force was launched some 170 miles south-east of the target. The third crew member, the TAG, was deleted in each aircraft due to the fitting of a 60gal overload (auxiliary) fuel tank. The first aircraft laid its magnesium flares at half-mile spacing along the line of the balloon barrage on the south-east side of the harbour. This provided back-lighting for the torpedo bombers.

Descending from 8,000ft the first wave of six Swordfish wove their way through the western balloon barrage and launched their Mark XII torpedoes from 30ft at ranges estimated at between 400 to 1,500yd. Running at a depth of about 32ft the torpedoes would have proceeded towards their targets at around 25kt.

A second wave of aircraft sped in five minutes after the first. These Swordfish pressed home their attacks even closer to their quarry, down to within 500–800yd. While the principal activity took place in the *Mare Grande* (the main harbour), part of the strike force attacked cruisers and destroyers in the *Mare Piccolo* (the smaller, inner anchorage), together with an oil storage depot and seaplane hangar.

In a sense the big warships, being moored in harbour, were quite helpless. Had they been under way, out at sea, their captains would

RIGHT Commissioned in February 1924, HMS *Eagle* was a carrier conversion of the Chilean battleship *Almirante Cochrane*. She boasted two storeys of hangar. However, even with this advantage she could accommodate no more than 24 aircraft. This, together with her modest maximum speed and limited flight deck dimensions, hampered her effectiveness in some fleet operations. *(Jonathan Falconer collection)*

Taranto Naval Base. The extensive provision of anti-aircraft batteries and the concentrated balloon barrage system can be seen in this map. It gives some idea of the challenges facing the Swordfish aircrews on the night of 10–11 November 1940. *(Crown Copyright)*

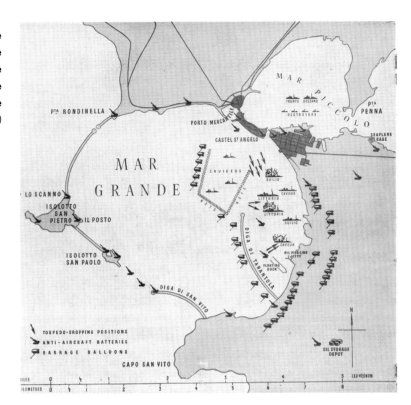

have practised the well-known manoeuvre of 'combing the tracks' to avoid torpedo runs. As it was they presented a much easier static target, silhouetted against the light of the flares. Sitting ducks one might say.

However, that is not to say the Swordfish aircrew's job was anything but terrifyingly dangerous. They were facing massed anti-aircraft fire with the pilots' scope for avoiding action constrained by the need to dodge balloon cables and ships' masts.

Eventually each pilot's attention would have been focussed on aiming his aircraft at its target and holding the aircraft down to the requisite height, which had to be around 30ft for there to be an effective torpedo launch – difficult things to judge even in daylight and under ideal conditions.

Nineteen Swordfish of the attacking force returned safely to their carrier. Only two aircraft were shot down, one piloted by Lt Cdr Williamson (the force leader) succeeded in releasing his torpedo to blow a 25ft hole in *Conte di Cavour* before crashing and being taken into captivity with his observer. The other machine crewed by Lt Bayley and Lt Slaughter was not seen again after being hit by AA fire. The night attack at Taranto exceeded all expectations and became the stuff of legend.

Reconnaissance photos the next day revealed the full extent of the damage wreaked at the naval base. *Conte di Cavour* had sunk and, though eventually raised, she never returned to service, having suffered irreparable keel damage. *Littorio* received damage from three torpedoes and would not see service for another four months. A similar fate befell *Caio Duilio*, beached after a massive explosion, which

Taranto before the attack. Six Italian Navy battleships are at anchor in the presumed safety of the Mar Grande at the naval base, on the day before the night attack. *(Crown Copyright)*

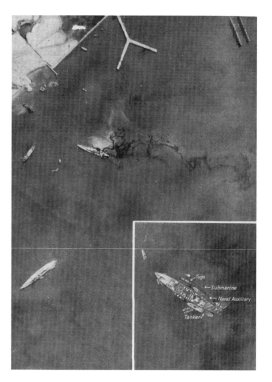

RIGHT Taranto – the aftermath. Three battleships have been hit by Swordfish torpedoes, with the *Italia* (the renamed *Littorio*), the *Caio Duilio* and the *Conte di Cavour*, if not sinking, then resting on the bottom or beached. The damage was such that *Italia* remained out of action for four months, *Caio Duilio* for six and *Cavour* never went to sea again. *(Crown Copyright)*

BELOW Skuas and Swordfish land on the deck of HMS *Ark Royal* after attacking the Italian Fleet during the action off Sardinia, 27 November 1940. Aesthetically evocative though this *contre jour* shot may be, it demonstrates quite convincingly how tempting and clear the famous aircraft carrier's high silhouette would be to an attacking German or Italian submarine, especially with the ship's attention focussed on landing-on activity. *(FAA Museum)*

required a similar extended period of repairs to her keel. The extent of destruction, particularly to hulls, would have been aided by the fitting of magnetic pistols to the British torpedoes.

Add to these achievements the mayhem caused in the inner harbour among anchored cruisers and destroyers, and the damage to oil tanks and the seaplane base, and it is possible to appreciate the magnitude of the effect this had on Italy's naval capability and its morale.

Ironically the Taranto attack took place around the time Italian bombers participated in a daylight raid on London, losing 13 aircraft.

There was indeed room for rejoicing in the Mediterranean Fleet. In just under an hour, for the loss of just two aircraft and two aircrew, the FAA had achieved more than the Grand Fleet at Jutland some quarter of a century before when 6,000 lives had been sacrificed.

Cap Spartivento, 27 November 1940

Responsibility for the protection of convoys carrying supplies and troop reinforcements through the Mediterranean in 1940 was divided between the Eastern Fleet stationed at Alexandria and Force H based at Gibraltar.

The eastward convoy which left Gibraltar on 25 November 1940 was escorted by Force H, commanded by Admiral Somerville, which included HMS *Ark Royal*. Reconnaissance by her aircraft revealed an Italian battle fleet south of Sardinia. A strike force of eleven Swordfish was launched from *Ark Royal*. The battleship *Vittorio Veneto* escaped unscathed. A second attack by nine aircraft against the Italian cruisers was also unsuccessful.

The double failure to secure any damage to the Italian ships led to an Admiralty Board of Inquiry. In the event Somerville was exonerated, but through this investigation and other evidence it became clear that the lack of torpedo hits was due in no small measure to the inadequate extent of aircrew training with this weapon.

The Tirso dam and Genoa raids, February 1941

Given the mobility conferred by their carriers it was not surprising the Royal Navy took every opportunity to strike at the Italian mainland. In the best traditions of 'carrying the battle to the enemy' one such example was the attempt by torpedo-armed Swordfish from HMS *Ark Royal* to break the Tirso dam on Sardinia. This was attacked on 2 February 1941. Weather conditions were against the operation, intelligence was weak and the dam stood up to the damage and failed to break up.

However, less than a week later, on 8 February, Swordfish from 818 NAS took part in a raid on the northern Italian port of La Spezia. The aircraft spotted for the guns of the battleship HMS *Barham* and the battle cruiser HMS *Renown* and bombed factories and laid mines at the entrance to La Spezia naval dockyard as well as bombing targets further afield at Pisa.

These mainland strike incursions are just a few of many that were undertaken by carrier-borne Swordfish along the eastern coast of Italy at this time. Unfortunately the vulnerability of capital ships to U-boat attack continued. HMS *Barham* succumbed to three U-boat torpedoes on 24 November 1941. Less than a fortnight before it had been the turn of the legendary and seemingly invincible carrier *Ark Royal*. The torpedoing of *Ark Royal* by *U81*

BELOW A view from HMS *Hermione* of the damaged and listing *Ark Royal* following her fatal wounding by torpedo strikes on 13 November 1941. The aircraft carrier was torpedoed by the German U-boat *U81* off Gibraltar and sank the following day. Mercifully casualty figures were very low; just one life lost. Due to inherent design faults and the resulting damage control decisions, the carrier eventually sank after efforts to tow her to Gibraltar had failed. Fortunately some of her Swordfish complement was able to reach North Front, Gibraltar, and in less than three days 812 NAS had begun anti-submarine patrols in the Straits. *(IWM A 6334)*

ASV RADAR

There is no doubt that the introduction of ASV (Air-to-Surface Vessel) radar on maritime aircraft had a dramatic effect on the war at sea. The move to centimetric equipment (sets using long-wave transmission with a longer range) came as a great shock to the enemy. Grand Admiral Dönitz in his memoirs expressed quite forcefully the frantic response of his Staff when it became clear U-boats were being surprised at night on the surface with very little warning.

The British version of ASV went through several marks. The Mark I version was initially installed in RAF Lockheed Hudson patrol aircraft in early 1940. Later the same year tests were carried out with an improved Mark II version and this went into service in 1941. In the case of this early mark ASV, the operator would be presented with a vertical scale marked off in nautical miles, with the echo signal shown as a 'blip' at its appropriate distance ahead of the aircraft. Later marks provided a pictorial representation of objects and/or terrain. Early airborne radar was characterised by aerial arrays on an aircraft's nose, fuselage and/or wings, depending on the airframe configuration. Early Swordfish installations can be identified by so-called 'Yagi' aerials, extending forwards and outwards from inter-plane struts.

The centimetric breakthrough came in 1942 when the change to a rotating scanner increased chances of aerial detection by a significant margin.

Fitting ASV Mark X precluded use of the aircraft in its torpedo attack role. Priorities had in any case changed. By late 1944 the threat posed by the large surface units of the German Navy had greatly diminished. The U-boat, however, remained a potent threat right until the very end of European hostilities. Prompt detection and effective dispatch, through rockets, bombs or depth charges, was the order of the day – a role the Fairey Swordfish discharged with extraordinary effect right up until 8 May 1945.

ABOVE A Swordfish Mark III with ASV Mark X in a 'Guppy'-type radome. Note that this aircraft is equipped with Rocket-Assisted Take-Off Gear (RATOG) located behind the lower wing roots. Also that slots are deployed on the leading edges of the upper mainplane. The equivalent US term for RATOG was Jet-Assisted Take-Off Gear (JATOG). The equipment came to be used where flight decks were short, aircraft were heavily loaded on take-off or if windless conditions were being experienced. *(FAA Museum)*

30 miles east of Gibraltar on the 12th of that month, while thankfully without human loss, resulted nevertheless in the loss of some of her Swordfish. However a residue of these aircraft along with Skuas was able to be reconstituted at Gibraltar and as 812 NAS they then performed an important role guarding the Straits.

Equipped by now with ASV radar, the night-flying capability of the aircraft came to the fore when performing these tasks. Five U-boats were damaged during December 1941 and the crews' efforts were eventually crowned with success on the night of 21–22 December when Type VIIC, *U541* (*Korvettenkapitän* Eberhard Hoffmann), was sunk off Tangier.

Cape Matapan, March 1941

Early in the spring of 1941 attention focussed on the eastern Mediterranean. At this point German forces had intervened in the Italian invasion of Greece. General Sir Archibald Wavell, Commander-in-Chief Middle East, was obliged to send British and Commonwealth troops to the Greek mainland in aid of his allies.

The transporting of 50,000 men and their equipment from Egypt to Greece, codenamed Operation 'Lustre', together with its protection at sea, posed a further responsibility for the Eastern Mediterranean Fleet. Its Commander-in-Chief, Admiral A.B. Cunningham, continued to maintain a watchful eye on the Italian

Navy, which was still smarting from the blow delivered at Taranto the previous November but recovering from its setbacks and regaining its confidence. Interception of troopship convoys by the Italians could have had tragic consequences.

In late March 1941, an Italian Fleet put to sea. Four heavy cruisers were escorted by several destroyers and the battleship *Vittorio Veneto* also accompanied this fleet as it sailed eastwards towards the Egypt–Greece convoy route.

Aerial contact was made on 27 March and an attack mounted next day by Albacores from HMS *Formidable*. This was unsuccessful. Swordfish of 815 NAS based at Maleme on Crete then attacked the cruisers *Trento* and *Bolzano* but this again was without any success. However, it fell to an Albacore from *Formidable* to resolve the problem posed by the Italian battleship, by hitting *Vittorio Veneto* with a well-aimed torpedo, below the waterline before itself hit by AA fire, it crashed. Nevertheless after hasty repairs, the battleship was able to make its escape from Cunningham's oncoming fleet.

In the event, of greater consequence was an attack in failing light by a joint force of *Formidable*'s Albacores and Maleme's Swordfish. One of the latter from 815 NAS succeeded in stopping the heavy cruiser *Pola* in her tracks with a torpedo hit in her engine room. What followed that night has always been regarded as the classic night action.

With the onset of darkness, the two sister ships of *Pola* returned to give her assistance. During this process, *Zara* and *Fiume* were surprised by the British Fleet. All three cruisers together with two destroyers were sunk by the guns of HMS *Warspite* and her sister battleships, with that ship's catapult-launched 700 NAS Swordfish floatplane aircraft spotting for their guns.

While this was principally a surface action, there is little doubt that this significant reduction of numbers of the Italian Fleet was wholly enabled through a well-aimed Swordfish torpedo strike.

However, of equal importance in terms of its effect on Italian morale, was the torpedo hit on *Veneto*, scored during the joint Swordfish/Albacore strike. While this only temporarily slowed the battleship, it served even further to create extreme wariness with the deployment

BELOW The ill-fated *Pola*, *Zara* and *Fiume* in port before the action at Cape Matapan. All three 8in-gunned Italian cruisers were sunk by the Royal Navy during the night action of 28 March 1941, off Cape Matapan. The sequence of events leading to their destruction was triggered by a well-aimed torpedo from an 815 NAS Swordfish. This crippled the *Pola* and led to her two sister ships fatally standing by to render assistance. *(Topham Picturepoint 2001)*

of Italian Navy capital ships when it was known that a British carrier was at sea.

A further joint attack followed, the strike force including two of 815's Swordfishes. One of these aircraft piloted by Torrens Spence was able to stop the cruiser *Pola*. On completion of the mission all aircraft were routed back to Crete and although aircraft were lost all aircrew taking part in the attack survived the sortie.

ATTACKS ON THE FRENCH FLEET, 1940

Churchill in his memoirs describes what happened to the French Fleet at its bases at Oran and Dakar as the result of 'a hateful decision, the most unnatural and painful in which I have ever been concerned'.

With the collapse of France as an independent nation in June 1940, the presence of a powerful French Fleet under Vichy control in the ports of Metropolitan France and her African colonies posed a major risk to British and Allied strategy in the Mediterranean and beyond.

Planning the neutralisation of this potential threat, took precedence over other naval matters in the summer of 1940. Force H, a powerful squadron of capital ships including an aircraft carrier, was henceforth based at Gibraltar. This move was intended to make up for the removal of the French Navy's contribution to the security of the western Mediterranean, as a result of the Armistice.

Oran and Mers-el-Kebir

Warned in advance that refusal to scuttle or disable their fleet at these naval bases would result in retaliatory force, no positive response was received from the newly installed Vichy-based French government by a deadline that was several times extended.

Force H was soon in action. Other diplomatic initiatives to neutralise the French Fleet having failed, Force H appeared off Mers-el-Kebir, the principal naval harbour adjoining Dakar, on 3 July 1940 and proceeded to attack the French North African port and the warships it sheltered.

The use of force in this way against a nation who only a short time before had been a close ally was both controversial and deeply repugnant to the senior Royal Navy staff that were committed to undertake it.

CATAPULT ASPECTS OF THE SWORDFISH

LEFT A dual Swordfish is launched off the catapult at Gosport. The provision of a small batch of dual-control trainers was followed up by similar adaptations of Fairey Battle and Firefly aircraft. *(Copyright unknown)*

Catapult research and development, which was centred on the RAE at Farnborough, resulted in a system that was capable of launching an aircraft every 40sec. Initially Royal Navy carriers used the well-tried trolley and track system. These were deployed in pairs on Fleet Carriers.

All-up weight was a critical factor. This constraint was built into manufacturers' specifications as were stress requirements. The Swordfish was designed for catapult launch from the outset. The fuselage with its cross bracing of steel tube and wire, was designed to accommodate the stresses it would undergo when subjected to the forces of the launch. Two spools, circular stressed projections along each side of the fuselage, provided points of attachment to the trolley on turntable-type catapults or in the case of flush carrier versions, attachment points for the strops which led down to slide.

Apart from training installations like the TTU at Gosport, catapults were installed in two locations on board ship. The first in fixed-bow positions on aircraft carriers for accelerated bow launches. These launches were particularly helpful when take-offs were subject to unfavourable wind conditions and/or when heavy weapons loads were being carried. Second was the swivelling catapult installations in beam positions used to launch Swordfish floatplanes from larger warships, mainly for spotting duties.

A small number of dual-control Swordfish were employed as catapult trainers, with training installations at stations like that at the TTU Gosport.

ABOVE Mers-el-Kebir, 3 July 1940: in the foreground is *Provence*, on the right *Strasbourg* leaving the anchorage, and in the background *Bretagne* on fire. The *Bretagne* subsequently blew up. Tragically around 1,300 French lives were lost in this saddest of naval actions. *Strasbourg*, however, shrugged off her pursuers and reached the safety of her base at Toulon after an unsuccessful attack by six Swordfish from HMS *Ark Royal*. During this action some of the aircraft flew as low as 20ft above the sea to secure the right entry for their torpedoes. *(Roger-Viollet/TopFoto)*

BELOW The French battleship *Dunkerque* was scuttled at Toulon in November 1942. She is seen here late in the war. Swordfish from *Ark Royal* had made an unsuccessful attempt to sink the battleship in July 1940 while she was disabled at Mers-el-Kebir. *Dunkerque,* having returned to Toulon and subsequent to the Allies landing in North Africa and the resultant seizure by the Germans of Vichy France, was among some 70 French naval ships that were deliberately sunk. *(Jonathan Falconer collection)*

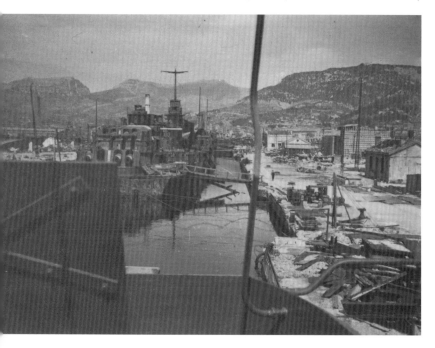

Force H's carrier played an important part in the proceedings. As her contribution to Operation 'Catapult', HMS *Ark Royal* flew off Swordfish aircraft from 810 NAS. These proceeded to mine the entrances to the harbour after which they provided spotting assistance for the guns of HMS *Hood*, HMS *Valiant* and HMS *Resolution*, as they steamed in line ahead just off shore.

In the ensuing bombardment the battleship *Bretagne* blew up with tragic loss of life and both the *Provence* and *Dunkerque* received serious damage.

Six Swordfish of 820 NAS mounted a torpedo strike against the beached *Dunkerque* three days later. During this attack, a lighter alongside the beached *Dunkerque* exploded causing further damage to the battle cruiser. Two further follow-up sorties, escorted this time by Skuas, were generally inconclusive but drew resistance from French Curtiss Hawk and Morane Saulnier fighters. In retrospect the lack of success, particularly with the torpedo, was put down to insufficient practice.

During their initial sorties the Swordfish were attacked by French Dewoitine fighters. These were more than a match for the TBRs, which only eluded their attackers by exploiting their slow speed and infinitely superior manoeuvrability.

During the turmoil the battleship *Strasbourg* and five destroyers escaped. Though attacked twice by six of *Ark*'s Swordfish en route, one sortie with bombs, the other with torpedoes, no hits were recorded, two aircraft were lost, and the ships eventually gained the safety of the French naval base.

Dakar, July 1940

Dakar, the French naval base on the West African coast, was the home port for *Richelieu,* the most modern of the French battleships. Its presence posed a dangerous threat to the Royal Navy. This factor coupled with the proximity of a Vichy French naval base on the Atlantic seaboard, served to place the capture or at least neutralisation of the port high on the British agenda.

A watch was kept on the movements of the French battleship. Having been shadowed by aircraft from HMS *Hermes* the *Richelieu* sought sanctuary with three destroyers at Dakar.

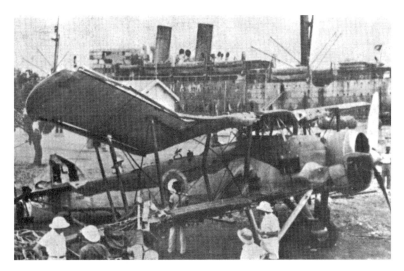

A torpedo strike against *Richelieu* in harbour was mounted from *Hermes* by 814 NAS on 8 July. It was pressed home against fierce AA fire and achieved some success. The ship sustained damage to its propulsion machinery. With the limited repair facilities available at Dakar this ensured it would not be fully serviceable for another year.

Further attacks on Dakar were then mounted by the Royal Navy two months later, as part of Operation 'Menace'. This was a Combined Operation attack involving over 6,500 British and Free French troops and was intended capture the port. During the course of this action, Force H warships were damaged while off the port. HMS *Barham* was hit by fire from *Richelieu* and the port's shore batteries, as were two British cruisers and a destroyer, and *Resolution* was torpedoed. French Martin Maryland bombers were also active. These problems, coupled with the failure to achieve further success against the ships in harbour, led to the abandonment of Operation 'Menace' on 26 September 1940, much to the chagrin of Churchill and the First Lord.

THE NORTH ATLANTIC
The Sinking of *Bismarck,* May 1941

The Royal Navy resumed the role in September 1939 that lay at the very heart of its existence, namely the defence of the sea lanes. Paradoxically devoid of the benefit of foresight, Admiralty concerns and priorities appear to have been principally focussed on the threat from what were termed surface raiders rather than on the build-up of the German U-boat arm. Surface raiding preyed on Allied merchant shipping during this early period of the war. In this regard the German Navy exploited the capabilities of a new type of warship specifically designed for this purpose, the pocket battleship. These units with their considerable range and powerful armament, of larger calibre

than the Royal Navy's heavy cruisers, posed a serious danger to merchant shipping.

Before being brought to account by ships of Group G, the South Atlantic Cruiser Squadron, off the River Plate, the German pocket battleship *Graf Spee* had been highly effective in this role. Furthermore, skirmishes between Royal Navy and German battle cruisers off Norway had reinforced the sober truth that mere superiority in numbers, which the Royal Navy possessed, was no guarantee that shipping lanes could be made secure.

Evidence gained from photographic reconnaissance on 21 May 1941 showed that two large units of the German Navy had made their way north from their Baltic base and

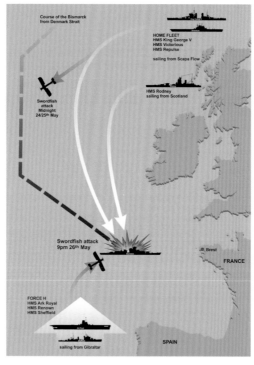

RIGHT The map shows the converging tracks of the Home Fleet and Force H units as they searched for and attacked the *Bismarck*. *(Roy Scorer)*

anchored in a Norwegian fjord. This report rang alarm bells at the Admiralty. Identification of the ships as the battleship *Bismarck*, at that time the most modern ship of its class in the world, accompanied by the heavy 8in cruiser *Prinz Eugen*, set emergency plans in motion. When as a result of a daring photo-reconnaissance sortie across Kors and Bergen Fjords it was confirmed the quarry had left, orders were issued to British naval units that this formidable force must be intercepted and sunk.

So important was this emergency that heavy Royal Navy warships were released from guarding convoys to tackle the two German warships. In particular the new armoured aircraft carrier, HMS *Victorious,* was detached from prospective duty giving protection for a Middle East troop convoy in order to provide the vital air component of the Royal Navy response. The aircraft carrier, still not fully worked up, left Scapa Flow late in the evening of 22 May. She was in company with the modern battleship HMS *King George V* and the rather aged battle cruiser HMS *Repulse,* together with an accompanying force of cruisers and destroyers, and carried nine Swordfish of 825 NAS.

However, before this quite formidable Home Fleet force had got within striking distance of the two German ships on the 24th, action had been joined by HMS *Prince of Wales* and HMS *Hood*, battleship and battle cruiser respectively. These had been sent ahead to intercept the raiders. Tragically *Hood* experienced a magazine explosion from expert German gunnery and sank at around 6.00pm with virtually all her crew lost.

LEFT *Bismarck* firing at HMS *Hood* during the action in the Denmark Strait. This photograph was taken from the *Prinz Eugen* on 24 May. This is the kind of formidable firepower that confronted *Ark Royal*'s Swordfish aircrews two days later during their attack on 26 May. *(IWM HU381)*

However, the second wave of naval forces was coming across from the east at last. On the evening of that fatal day, *Victorious* launched all nine of her Swordfish aircraft. Due to hangar space being given over to fighters destined for Malta her TSR complement had been reduced. These aircraft were dispatched in the late evening under the command of Lt Cdr Eugene Esmonde (later to be awarded a posthumous VC for the attack on the two German battle cruisers during what came to be known as the 'Channel Dash'). This first sortie benefited from ASV (see Glossary).

The attack went in. Torpedoes were released by all the Swordfish around midnight. At least one hit was observed. Though this struck the battleship's armoured belt, it is believed this led to an exacerbation of the damage to the *Bismarck*'s oil tanks inflicted by *Prince of Wales* in the previous encounter. All Swordfish were recovered although not without difficulty, with D/F bearings having to be given by the carrier, which also used its searchlight to home in its flock.

The fuel problem may have turned out in the end to have been a critical factor. This could have led Admiral Günther Lütjens, the German commander, to call off Operation 'Rheinübung' as the Kriegsmarine foray was called. He decided to dispatch *Prinz Eugen* to operate independently before making her way home separately. He himself set course for Brest, the German-held port on the coast of France. The need to conserve fuel meant that the ship reduced speed. However, as it happened this change of course played to *Bismarck*'s advantage insofar as the shadowing Royal Navy cruisers straightaway lost touch with her. This was when Home Fleet warships were no more than 100 miles from the German battleship. As a result the Home Fleet squadron continued in a south-westerly direction, away from their quarry.

Nevertheless, after more than 24 hours of this kind of cat-and-mouse chase, contact with the ship was eventually regained. On the morning of 26 May *Bismarck* was spotted by a patrolling RAF Catalina flying boat. It then became clear she was heading on a south-easterly course towards Brest. The Home Fleet units were at this time still heading south-west on a false trail. They had little chance of catching up.

Notwithstanding the Home Fleet's errors

LIEUTENANT COMMANDER (A) JOHN MOFFAT, RNVR

LEFT John Moffat, the author of *I sank the Bismarck* and one of the very last survivors of that most dramatic episode in British naval history. Born in Scotland he grew up in the Border country and followed his father into the Royal Navy. By coincidence his father served on the *Ark*'s name predecessor in the First World War. *(Copyright unknown)*

John Moffat was one of fifteen FAA pilots who took off in their Swordfish from HMS *Ark Royal* at 14:15hrs on 26 May 1941, their mission, to attack the German battleship *Bismarck*. He was in the first sub-flight to launch torpedoes at the German battleship. This and subsequent attacks resulted in critical damage to the steering machinery of the vessel enabling the British Fleet to secure her end. Remarkably all aircraft returned to their carrier despite damage to aircraft and two wounded aircrew.

Writing many years after the event, John Moffat recalled the momentous events of those two days of action on 26 and 27 May. He was fulsome in his praise for the Swordfish. He firmly believed no other aircraft could have achieved what the Swordfishes did on that blustery day, way out in the Atlantic with a Force 8 gale in progress and the carrier deck pitching 60ft with the motion of the sea. He went on to affirm his faith in the toughness of the Swordfish. He had some 400 hours of flying experience on them and can remember during the *Bismark* attack surviving with most of the lower wing and under fuselage fabric shot away and with his fuel tank embedded with shrapnel.

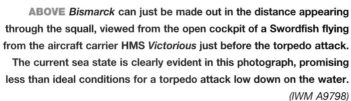

ABOVE *Bismarck* can just be made out in the distance appearing through the squall, viewed from the open cockpit of a Swordfish flying from the aircraft carrier HMS *Victorious* just before the torpedo attack. The current sea state is clearly evident in this photograph, promising less than ideal conditions for a torpedo attack low down on the water. *(IWM A9798)*

ABOVE RIGHT Swordfish of 825 NAS on the afterdeck of HMS *Victorious* before the attack on the *Bismarck* on the evening of 24 May. Note the lowered arrester wire in the foreground and the slippery conditions that obtained on the flight deck. *(FAA Museum)*

BELOW A pall of black smoke rises from *Bismarck* after an attack by Swordfish from *Victorious*. The Swordfish struck around midnight on 24 May. Only one hit was confirmed. This exploded relatively harmlessly on *Bismarck*'s protective armoured belt, despite the black cloud that was emitted by the ship. *(FAA Museum)*

BELOW RIGHT A Swordfish from *Ark Royal* returns at low level over the sea after making a torpedo attack on *Bismarck*. The empty torpedo crutch signifies delivery of its weapon. *(FAA Museum)*

of judgement, help was at hand. Force H had come up from Gibraltar and in the event its participation effectively turned the tables on *Bismarck*. Aboard the Force's aircraft carrier HMS *Ark Royal* were the Swordfish of 810, 818 and 820 NAS.

Having first been sighted on the morning of 26 May, *Bismarck* was now within range of carrier aircraft again. Accordingly throughout the evening of that day Swordfish aircraft from *Ark Royal* shadowed her in relays, clinging to her like leaches. Two strikes were mounted during the course of that day. The first comprised 14 aircraft, the second 15. All Swordfish were armed with torpedoes and ASV was installed in one of the aircraft. The first strike was launched in the early afternoon in particularly bad weather. This sortie was bedevilled by mistaken identity, the force attacking HMS *Sheffield* the shadowing cruiser by mistake. However, the second attempt in the early evening turned out,

arguably, to be the most decisive of the whole three days of *Bismarck* action. A single torpedo hit damaged the ship's steering gear and propellers. This forced the battleship to reduce her speed drastically and she was only able to steer an erratic course.

Thus it was that the FAA effectively delivered the pride of the German Navy on to the guns of the British battle fleet. There could only be one outcome to such an encounter.

As a final sortie of *Ark*'s Swordfish arrived over the stricken ship the next morning; their crews were in time to see the cruiser *Dorsetshire* deliver the *coup de grâce* with torpedoes. Hopelessly outnumbered by Royal Navy ships, she had been battered to a hulk by the 16in guns of *Rodney*. Witnessing the last moments of *Bismarck* as she up-ended and went down, with Ensign still flying there was nothing more for the *Ark Royal*'s aircrew to do but jettison their torpedoes and return to their carrier. The time was 10:36hrs on the morning of 27 May 1941.

Following on the overwhelming success of Taranto, some six months previously, it was now clear to those sceptical of naval airpower, that its skilful deployment, using the unique qualities of the TSR Swordfish to the full, could almost turn the tide of the war at sea at a stroke. What both torpedo engagements also established was that disablement, although less spectacular than outright sinking, could deliver results that were ultimately as dramatic and successful in tactical and strategic terms as more impressive outcomes.

Norway, July 1941
Operation 'Barbarossa', the German invasion of Russia in the summer of 1941, drew a quick response by the Royal Navy. As a British gesture of support, carrier-borne aircraft attacked the German-occupied ports of Kirkenes and Petsamo in northern Norway. The carriers HMS *Furious* and *Ark Royal* supplied the aircraft, with Albacores from the latter ship and Swordfish of 812 NAS carrying out strikes on ships and harbour installations, escorted by Fulmars from both carriers.

Flak and German fighters took a heavy toll of the Albacores at Kirkenes. Eleven were shot down, although a freighter was sunk and another severely damaged.

The Swordfish fared rather better at Petsamo

with one torpedo sinking a small steamer and with shore installations damaged.

Operation 'Fuller' – The 'Channel Dash', February 1942
Two major challenges faced the Royal Navy in early 1942. The powerful new German battleship *Tirpitz* had taken up station in Norway and far away to the south a powerful squadron of warships comprising the battle cruisers *Scharnhorst* and *Gneisenau* and the heavy 8in cruiser *Prinz Eugen* lay at Brest on the Brittany peninsula awaiting the opportunity to sail back to their bases in northern Germany.

This eventuality had been foreseen and plans had been in place for some time. Operation 'Fuller' called for co-ordinated RAF and Royal Navy attacks on any such excursion by surface vessels and by aircraft.

Unfortunately a series of errors and mishaps bedevilled the monitoring by the British of the movements of this very powerful Brest-based Kriegsmarine squadron. ASV radar failure on shadowing RAF Hudson aircraft, enemy radar jamming and over-meticulous observance of W/T silence all played a part in inhibiting the British response to the break-out late in the evening of 11 February. These factors and others such as murky weather in the English Channel conspired to mask the Channel Dash of these ships in their attempt to regain their north German bases.

By the time the alarm had been raised the ships were well up the Channel. No 825 NAS, commanded by the veteran of the *Bismarck* attacks Lt Cdr Eugene Esmonde, was activated

ABOVE The German battlecruisers *Scharnhorst* and *Gneisenau* travel in a line with their guns firing, allegedly pictured during their escape from Brest in what has become known as the 'Channel Dash' on 12 February 1942. While both ships eventually succumbed to some damage en route from aerially laid mines, the combined efforts of naval forces, including destroyers and MTBs, Coastal Command aircraft, shore batteries and (tragically) six FAA Swordfish, failed to prevent the two battle cruisers and their escorts making safe haven at their north German bases. *(IWM MH4981)*

ABOVE Lt Cdr Eugene Esmonde was awarded a posthumous Victoria Cross for his attack on the *Scharnhorst* and *Gneisenau* in the Dover Straits on 12 February 1942 while his squadron (825) was based at HMS *Daedalus* (RNAS Lee-on-the-Solent). All six Swordfish that took part were shot down with their eighteen aircrew. There were just five survivors, three of whom were injured in the attack. He is seen here with officers and ratings that were decorated for their part in the sinking of the *Bismarck*, in front of a Swordfish aircraft. Left to right: Lt P.D. Gick, RN (awarded the DSC); Lt Cdr Eugene Esmonde, RN (awarded the DSO); Sub Lt V.K. Norfolk, RN (awarded the DSC); A/PO Air L.D. Sayer (awarded the DSM); A/Ldg Air A.L. Johnson (awarded the DSM). *(FAA Museum)*

ABOVE Operation 'Ironclad', which led to the capture of the Vichy French-held island of Madagascar in May 1942, was a Combined Operation that involved units of all three services. Three 810 NAS Swordfish from HMS *Illustrious* dropped a total of eighteen dummy parachutists as a diversion, successfully deceiving the Vichy authorities into believing that an airborne attack was under way. *(Copyright unknown)*

just after noon on 12 February. The squadron Swordfish were already on station at RAF Manston in Kent, having been ordered there at the beginning of the month. Despite the recognition that a minimum force of around ten aircraft was needed to at least cripple a capital ship, Esmonde accepted the unevenness of the confrontation and the six aircraft flying in two sub-flights took off at 12:30hrs heading for the Calais area. Two Biggin Hill-based RAF Spitfire fighter squadrons provided some cover. However, the Luftwaffe fighters were out in force and swamped the RAF escorts. As a result these became detached from the FAA machines. All three Swordfish in the first wave were shot down, with Esmonde killed when launching his torpedo after a strike by a Focke-Wulf Fw190 fighter. Five out of the nine aircrew in this first wave survived. The crews of the three second-wave aircraft were not so lucky. All were shot down and killed while pressing home their attacks.

Esmonde's decision to attack the German squadron has been criticised over the years, but undoubtedly it was made bearing in mind the very best traditions of the Service and its air arm.

INDIAN OCEAN
Operation 'Ironclad', Madagascar, May 1942

After the highly destructive forays of the Imperial Japanese Navy into the Indian Ocean in April 1942, which saw the sinking of the carrier HMS *Hermes* and the cruiser HMS *Dorsetshire*, attention focussed on the French possession of Madagascar. This large island off the coast of East Africa posed a potential threat to troop convoys and commercial traffic in the Indian Ocean through its loyalty to the Vichy government. A Combined Operations assault was mounted on the north of the island close to the important deep-water harbour of Diego Suarez. Operation 'Ironclad' was commanded by Admiral Syfret and involved support from two Fleet Carriers HMS *Illustrious* and HMS *Indomitable*. At dawn on 5 May, Swordfish from *Illustrious*'s 810 and 829 NAS attacked French naval vessels, sinking the sloop *Entrecasteaux* and the armed cruiser *Bougainville*. Further success followed, the French submarines *Beveziers* and *Le Heros* falling victim to attack by the Swordfish of 829 NAS. Swordfish were also tasked with one of the more bizarre operations of the campaign, which involved the dropping of dummy parachutists as a deception.

Swordfish also spotted for the guns of the Fleet. Air superiority favoured the Swordfish strikes. Fortunately the timing of Operation 'Ironclad' coincided with the Battle of the Coral Sea, which ensured the absence of Imperial Japanese naval units who would have tipped the balance considerably.

Shore-based operations

By their nature carrier operations in the Second World War often required the movement of embarked squadrons to shore bases from time to time. Docking, refits and repairs prompted these relocations. More seriously, Swordfish NAS might require being shore-based if their parent ship suffered severe damage or indeed was sunk.

Given the stretched resources of the RAF, particularly in the Mediterranean during the period 1940–42, it is not surprising their commanders should seek any opportunity to enlist additional help. A pool of experienced

naval aircrew and their machines was seen as a way of complementing their own limited squadron strengths.

Thus we see Swordfish squadrons and their aircraft in action all round the Mediterranean, from bases in the Western Desert, Rhodes, Crete and Malta, all to aid their hard-pressed RAF colleagues and in turn to assist ground forces as they attempted to stem German advances in the eastern Mediterranean and along the North African coast.

With the Eastern Mediterranean Fleet based at Alexandria and the campaign in the Western Desert taking place along the North African coast, it was perhaps inevitable that NAS Swordfish would be called upon to aid Allied military and naval forces from land bases. As examples of this role, 824 NAS Swordfish from HMS *Eagle*, flying from Sidi Barrani, attacked Italian ships in Bomba harbour in August 1940, sinking two submarines, a destroyer and a depot ship without loss. Subsequently 824 NAS saw action in Greece during March 1941.

No 815 NAS was based for a short while at Maleme on Crete. From here they participated in the night action off Matapan, which led to the sinking of the three Italian heavy cruisers.

In late October 1940, having disembarked to Dekheila near Alexandria, 16 Swordfish from 814, 815 and 819 NAS flew west and after an intermediate stop launched an attack on Tobruk, dropping bombs and planting mines in the harbour entrance.

During the Abyssinian campaign Swordfish

LEFT Swordfish V4436, 'M', of 815 NAS in North Africa on anti-submarine duties carrying flares and depth charges. Land-based Swordfish made a valuable contribution to victory in the Western Desert and North African campaigns. Their anti-submarine capabilities, especially in radar-aided night operations, were recognised throughout the Second World War. *(Philip Jarrett collection)*

from 813 and 824 NAS were detached from Egypt to the Red Sea. Based at Port Sudan, they achieved considerable success. Their final tally was five Italian destroyers sunk, abandoned or scuttled.

During the Iraqi Revolt in May 1941 the aircraft of 814 NAS operated from shore bases in the Persian Gulf, providing support for ground forces by attacking Iraqi troops, stores and buildings.

Swordfish based on Malta created an enviable strike record during the three years 1940-43. No 830 NAS, the principal FAA squadron based at Hal Far, together with 828 NAS with its Albacores, sank an astonishing total of 400,000 tons of enemy shipping, with the lion's share going to the Swordfish formations.

The value of anti-shipping strikes from Malta cannot be overemphasised. It is no exaggeration to say that Allied successes in the campaign in the Western Desert would not have been possible without the continuous harassment of the Axis convoys, resulting in the destruction of material and equipment as well as personnel.

By the time 830 and 828 NAS were relieved by 826 NAS in 1943 they had created an enviable record of attacks on ports and shipping, including much success with their main weapon the torpedo.

Swordfish operations with the RAF

The year 1940 saw an arrangement between the Admiralty and the Air Ministry whereby a small number of NAS operated directly under RAF control as an integral part of RAF Coastal Command. Initially, Swordfish aircraft were tasked with mine-laying and anti-E-boat patrols.

No 815 NAS operated out of RAF Bircham Newton in Norfolk in these roles.

The start of the German Blitzkreig offensive on 10 May 1940 saw 815 NAS in action in the ground-attack role flying out of RAF Detling, Kent. No 825 NAS followed suit, bombing and machine-gunning enemy vehicles and troop concentrations as well as spotting for cruiser bombardments, attacking invasion barges and mine-laying off Channel estuaries. Seven Swordfish from the squadron even bombed Waalhaven airfield near Rotterdam.

Generally, from this point on, the squadron was involved in a whole host of activities along the Channel and inland, with anti-U-boat patrols not the least important activity. No 812 NAS also undertook a similar range of tasks, all under the control of RAF Coastal Command.

Later on in 1942 when the Navy's carrier requirements permitted, four Swordfish NAS were assigned to RAF Coastal Command. At this point the distinctive matt-black finish came to be adopted with 811 NAS as one of the first FAA units to use this night-camouflage scheme. The now well-established night anti-shipping operations continued with Swordfish regularly setting off from RAF stations at Thorney Island, Bircham Newton and Manston.

The legendary flexibility of the machine was underlined further on D-Day, 6 June 1944, when 816 NAS Swordfish laid smokescreens to provide cover for the invasion fleet. Anti-shipping sorties by the Coastal Command NAS continued after D-Day. The swansong of the Swordfish probably came about during a short period of RAF squadron service. Impressed by the machine's inherent qualities, not least its load carrying capability and night performance, the RAF had re-formed 119 Squadron at RAF Manston on 19 July 1944 from the Albacore Flight of 415 Squadron. In January 1945 it took on its first Swordfish Mark III aircraft and from then on patrols were flown up the Channel and into the North Sea.

Convoy duties

Swordfish participated in convoy work from the outset of the Second World War. This came about as a result of Fleet Carriers like HMS *Eagle* and *Ark Royal* being deployed to guard important Mediterranean convoys such as those to Malta, with their Swordfish complements flying anti-submarine patrols to protect the Fleet and their merchantmen.

However, with the coming of the Escort Carriers with their responsibility for guarding merchant ships on the vulnerable Gibraltar, North Atlantic and Arctic convoy routes, the Swordfish came into its own as a critical escort component, principally deployed in its anti-submarine role.

Two factors delayed the entry into service of the Escort Carriers with their Swordfish complements. First, the period from late 1942 to early 1943 saw Allied naval resources heavily committed to Operation 'Torch', the landings in north and north west Africa; and second, the early American-built ships suffered losses due to faults that resulted in one (HMS *Avenger*) readily succumbing to torpedoing and the other (HMS *Dasher*) blowing up due to inadequate aviation fuel safety provisions, all of which required modification in British shipyards before return to service.

North Atlantic and Gibraltar convoys

Looking first at the North Atlantic convoy situation, it was not until April 1943 that the first Escort Carrier on station, HMS *Biter,* with a complement of 811 NAS Swordfish, took up duties on the North Atlantic convoy routes.

HMS *Biter*'s embarked aircraft quickly proved their worth with 811's Swordfish sharing the sinking of two U-boats (*U203* and *U89*) with surface escort ships in late April and early May 1943. The period from April to June is generally recognised as being the turning point for Allied fortunes in what came to be called the Battle of the Atlantic.

ABOVE Swordfish V4448 of 833 NAS seen in September 1942 during Operation 'Torch'. British carrier aircraft were given American-style markings during this operation, the joint series of landings along the North African coast. This measure was adopted in anticipation of the considerable animosity that might be aroused among the Vichy French forces if they were confronted with the sight of British markings. *(FAA Museum)*

BELOW An aerial view of the 'Avenger'-class Escort Carrier HMS *Biter* from one of her Swordfish just after taking off. *Biter* was a veteran of the North Atlantic and Gibraltar convoys, escorting no less than 16 of them. She carried between 6 and 11 Swordfish along with her Wildcat complement. Success attended her anti-submarine operations on Atlantic convoy duty during the successive months of April and May 1944, when 811 NAS Swordfish shared with surface escorts the sinking of *U203* and *U89*. *(IWM A22715)*

ABOVE Merchant ships of Convoy JW53 pass through pack ice. This Russia-bound convoy has encountered an additional hindrance to those posed by enemy attacks. Those merchant ships allocated to a subsequent convoy (JW55B) and their escorts were threatened by no less an adversary than the German battle cruiser *Scharnhorst*. *(IWM A15360)*

BELOW Continual sweeping of the snow-covered flight deck on board HMS *Fencer* was necessary to keep it serviceable for the operation of aircraft during convoys to Russia. Two Swordfish aircraft of 842 NAS can be seen at the far end of the flight deck. Note the arrester cables stretched across the deck. *Fencer*'s 842 NAS Swordfish had the distinction of sinking three U-boats, *U277*, *U674* and *U959*, on two successive days in May 1944. *(IWM A23575)*

Escort Carriers with their Swordfish NAS also played a major part in the Gibraltar convoys. From May 1943 to August/September 1944 frequent movements were made of troops, equipment and supplies from the UK for the land campaigns in the Mediterranean. Seven Escort Carriers were operating on convoy escort duties by the end of 1943, all with Swordfish embarked, with the aircraft undertaking many anti-submarine searches from their Escort Carriers during this period.

Arctic convoys

With the North Atlantic sphere of operations taking priority, it was not until February 1944 that Swordfish-equipped Escort Carriers took part in the escorting of convoys to north Russia. At this point HMS *Chaser* accompanied both outward and return trips. These first voyages were very successful with Swordfish of the embarked 816 NAS sharing the sinking of *U472* on 4 March, following this up when acting alone with the destruction of *U366* on the 5th and *U973* on the 6th. The following month saw more Swordfish successes with 819 NAS participating with Grumman Avengers in the sinking of *U288* and involvement in causing serious damage to three more German submarines. The four Arctic convoys that followed saw the destruction of seven U-boats, with HMS *Fencer*'s 842 NAS sinking *U277*, *U674* and *U959* on two successive days in early March 1944.

The success of the presence of the Escort Carrier combination can be judged by the fact that during nine return trips to Russia in this period, over 300 merchant ships were safely escorted to their destinations with only four sinkings.

The final seven return Arctic convoys towards the end of 1944 and the months leading up to VE-Day in 1945, were all escorted by Escort Carriers. No 825 NAS Swordfish on HMS *Vindex* scored notable successes in August and September 1944, sharing in the sinking of *U344* and *U394*, and destroying unaided *U354*.

HMS *Campania* rounded off the FAA's U-boat account with her 813 NAS sinking *U921* and *U365* in convoys sailing during August and December, respectively.

Overall some 700 merchant ships were escorted in 27 Escort Carrier-accompanied Arctic convoys, with only 8 losses and a toll of 14 U-boats destroyed.

MAC ships represented the ultimate attempt to ensure that aircraft supported convoys. The first joined its convoy in May 1943 and in the space of a year there were 18 deployed on North Atlantic and Arctic convoys. Only Swordfish were embarked with these ships. They all retained their Merchant Navy identity and the aircraft were drawn from 836, 840 and 860 NAS of the Royal Netherlands Navy.

Although not credited with any U-boat kills, Swordfish on the MAC ships performed a valuable task in warding off likely U-boat attacks. No convoys accompanied by MAC ships suffered any sinkings and by September 1944 it was possible to withdraw them and their larger Escort Carrier sisters from the North Atlantic altogether.

Anti-submarine Swordfish

The effectiveness of the Swordfish as an enemy submarine hunter-killer, but especially of German U-boats, was derived from three main factors:

First, the development of effective anti-submarine weapons. It must be remembered that its principal weapon had been the torpedo, of little use against U-boats; second, the provision of an adequate seagoing platform from which to

BELOW Rocket-armed Swordfish take off from HMS *Tracker* for an armed sweep and anti-submarine patrol in the North Atlantic. While generally of limited dimensions, the 82ft width of the Escort Carrier's flight deck did permit the Swordfish to take off past other half-folded machines. *(Copyright unknown)*

operate far out at sea; and third, equipment with which to undertake the critical search and find stages of the anti-submarine mission.

So far as weapons were concerned the FAA and the RAF began the war with the almost wholly ineffective 100lb, 250lb and 500lb anti-submarine bombs, all of which could be carried by the Swordfish. Ineffective, because sinking a submarine with any kind of bomb required a combination of skill and luck that rarely came together.

The breakthrough came with the adoption of a modified type of standard Mark VII naval depth charge, principally of 250lb size. Swordfish would carry up to four of these very effective anti-submarine weapons. Filled eventually with Torpex, more powerful than previous types of explosive, and fitted with a depth pistol, when properly delivered these weapons spelled death and destruction for U-boats and their crews. The aim was to straddle the submarine with the depth charges, ideally as the U-boat was commencing its dive. The U-boat response to ASV guided attacks was to fight it out on the surface. Consequently, where they were available, Swordfish would be joined by FAA Wildcats or Sea Hurricanes that would distract the flak gunners on the submarines while the attacking Swordfish went about their business.

Following the success of tests that were carried out by Swordfish, rocket projectiles were added to the Swordfish armoury during 1943. In fact a Swordfish was the first aircraft to sink a U-boat when one from HMS *Archer's* 819 NAS destroyed *U752* on 23 May that year. The 25lb armour-piercing version of the standard rocket projectile was quite capable of piercing a U-boat's double-skinned pressure hull.

Again the attack would be significantly aided by the presence of a FAA fighter to add their weight of machine gun or cannon fire.

The addition of rocket projectiles prompted the introduction of the Swordfish Mark II with its reinforced and metal-clad lower mainplanes to cope with the behavioural characteristics of the new weapons.

Second, as has been already indicated, seagoing platforms were necessary if submarine attacks were to be suppressed. The entry into service of the Escort Carriers, followed later on by the MAC ships, met that need. Anti-submarine search-and-kill operations were significantly enhanced where the carriers were able to embark fighters. This was also true on the rare occasions when two carriers were attached to the convoy, thus adding to the aircraft and crews that could be deployed.

Finally, the anti-submarine capability of the Swordfish was greatly improved by the provision of ASV radar. As the culmination of successive fits, Marks X and XI gave the aircraft an advantage over its rival successor, the Grumman Avenger. The H2S scanner in its radome was a significant improvement on what had gone before. Fortuitously the fixed undercarriage configuration of the Swordfish lent itself to the fitting of what was quite a bulky installation. It is arguable whether at times the penalties imposed on engine and airframe almost outweighed the benefits conferred by the equipment. Slow already, the approach speed of a Swordfish lining up for an attack, with the extra weight and induced drag, might not exceed 90mph, even with relatively still air conditions. Since speed of attack was of the essence in tackling U-boats that were often capable of achieving a good speed on the surface, this might have proved an insurmountable handicap in some instances.

Perhaps the full benefit of the combination of weaponry and radar carried by the Swordfish became apparent when, during the last four months of the war in 1945, two shore-based RAF squadrons undertook night operations in the English Channel and North Sea. They were effective in sealing the fate of small German surface vessels of the E and R types and midget submarines that were active, particularly along the Dutch Coast, during that period.

Operating initially from RAF Manston but later on from B83/Knokke le Zoute in Belgium, 119 Squadron was equipped with ASV-fitted all-black camouflaged Mark IIIs. Patrols began with these aircraft in February 1945, the principal targets being E-boats and the German Navy's new 'last ditch' weapon the Biber (or midget) submarine. No 119 Squadron's Swordfish operated alongside those of 819 NAS right through to VE-Day.

The Royal Navy began the Second World War with seven Fleet Carriers, all of which operated the Swordfish. HMS *Furious*, *Courageous* and *Glorious* had been converted from the hull up, out of First World War battle cruisers. HMS *Argus* and *Eagle* were also conversions, while HMS *Hermes* had been constructed from the keel up as a small purpose-built carrier. HMS *Ark Royal*, newly commissioned at the war's outbreak, was a major departure from all previous designs and represented the shape of things to come.

The Royal Navy suffered serious ship losses in the first three years of the Second World War. By the end of 1942 all but *Furious* and *Argus* had been sunk. By that time four new ships of vastly improved design were in service but Swordfish numbers were significantly depleted when aircraft went down with their ships.

The new carriers, HMS *Victorious*, *Illustrious*, *Formidable* and *Indomitable* evolved from the *Ark Royal* design, but with fully armoured deck and armour protection to hangars and other vital parts. These were followed by HMS *Implacable* and *Indefatigable* with further minor improvements. All the armoured carriers were capable of speeds slightly in excess of 30kt.

ABOVE One of the first ships to be given a completely flush flight deck, *Argus* was principally employed on training and trials duties during its service. However, it did have its moment of glory in August 1940 when the veteran carrier, described by Admiral Somerville as 'a millstone round my neck' because of its low maximum speed, launched 16 Hurricanes to fly to assist in the defence of Malta. *(Jonathan Falconer collection)*

BELOW HMS *Eagle* pictured at sea in March 1942. Some five months later on 11 August *Eagle* was torpedoed and sunk by U73. However, by that time she and her squadrons had proved their worth by assisting in the Taranto raid and she had ferried more than 180 Spitfires to Malta. *(IWM A7840)*

The seven armoured-deck ships were true Fleet Carriers, able to act independently or provide the air arm of a main battle fleet. The penalty imposed by armour protection was the reduction in the number of aircraft that could be carried and launched. Whereas 70 could be embarked in *Ark Royal* with her two hanger decks, numbers were down to a maximum of around 40 in *Illustrious* and her sister ships.

Escort Carriers

As the war at sea progressed it became clear to the Admiralty that the effectiveness of the naval air arm, particularly in its convoy escort duties, was being seriously inhibited by the lack of carriers. Much smaller ships that took far less time to build were clearly the answer. Such vessels could be invaluable where specific duties, such as convoy escort, could be adequately performed by fewer shipborne aircraft than those carried by the large Fleet Carriers.

ABOVE Swordfish Mark II, HS545, 'B', in flight, probably while serving with 824 NAS during 1943–44. HS545's war duties included Atlantic convoy escort with the Escort Carrier HMS *Striker* in 1943, followed by Arctic convoys to the Kola Inlet in the Soviet Union with HMS *Vindex* in February 1944. The NASs embarked on *Vindex* had an enviable record of U-boat sinkings: between March and September 1944 the squadrons' Swordfish participated in the destruction of five U-boats while on escort duty and during anti-submarine sweeps. *(IWM TR118)*

The first British attempt at an Auxiliary Carrier, as they were briefly called, was the *Audacity*. She was converted from a captured German merchantman and was equipped with six Grumman Martlet fighters, proving her worth on the Gibraltar run over a four-month period. The carrier had no Swordfish embarked, but her Martlet aircraft were particularly successful against shadowing aircraft like the Focke-Wulf Fw200 Condor – the so called 'Scourge' – seven of which were shot down by aircraft from the ship.

No other British-built Auxiliary Carriers were to enter service until early 1944 when *Activity*, *Nairana*, *Vindex* and *Campania* became available for escort duties. Plans to convert liners resulted in one larger carrier, the *Pretoria Castle*, used mainly for trials.

US-supplied Escort Carriers

As happened with many innovations during wartime the US Navy was also exploring the potential for small auxiliary or 'Woolworth' aircraft carriers. The USS *Long Island* went into service at almost the same time as HMS *Audacity*. The first American versions supplied to the Royal Navy were based on a standard Maritime Commission C3 hull. The flight deck measured 495ft by 78ft and was provided with a single lift. Aircraft complement was 9 Swordfish and 6 Wildcats.

BELOW Maintenance crew bring a torpedo-loaded Swordfish of 835 NAS on to the flight deck of HMS *Battler* by hydraulic lift on 13 May 1943. The Escort Carrier's island can be seen in the background. *Battler*, an 'Attacker'-class Lend-Lease carrier, was fortunate in having the extended hangar of its class, which allowed up to a dozen Swordfish to be carried undercover. It was also furnished with two lifts and a single catapult (US – accelerator) on the port side. *(FAA Museum)*

HMS *Archer* (US Long Island class) was one of the first US-built Escort Carrier conversions, originally ordered for the US Navy but transferred to the Royal Navy. She was followed between November 1941 and July 1942 by three 'Avenger'-class carriers (modified US 'Long Island' class) *Avenger, Biter* and *Dasher*. Two of the class were lost through explosions so subsequent US-built Escort Carriers were modified to comply with Admiralty requirements. Modifications included extra ballast provision for stability and safety improvements for stowage of fuel and ordnance in the ship.

The Royal Navy received eleven of an improved C3 hull-based carrier, named the 'Attacker' class, between October 1942 and June 1943. Significantly this was the period of crisis for the Allies with their Atlantic convoys, the breakthrough being achieved in May 1943. Twelve Swordfish and six Martlets could be accommodated in a hangar with the extra help of lifts at both ends. A catapult or accelerator was another welcome addition.

The final third batch of 22 ships, were generally known as the 'Ruler' class. By this time the ships were built from the keel up as carriers. The 'Rulers', starting with HMS *Ameer*, incorporated further improvements over the two previous series. Hangars were larger and flight decks at 438ft were some 20ft longer than the 'Archers' enabling up to 20 aircraft to be embarked.

The US-supplied carriers proved their worth in many respects. Not only did they perform well in their trade protection role, assisting in the final defeat of the U-boat threat to convoys, but they also served to ferry aircraft, and within certain limits acted as close support vessels at amphibious landings, the so-called Assault Carriers. Finally and fittingly, during their last days of Royal Navy service, they acted as makeshift troopships bringing home service personnel and in particular POWs, from overseas theatres.

MAC ships

Faced with the delayed arrival of the main force of Escort Carriers from the US, the Admiralty looked around for a quicker solution based on the straight conversion of merchantmen. The result was the Merchant Aircraft Carrier or 'MAC ship'. Small cargo ships were looked at and two types were eventually chosen, grain carriers and oil tankers. Their suitability stemmed from the fact that their cargos could be pumped from holds, thus dispensing with the need for hatches. Grain ships were provided with a lift and hangar. These two alterations added some 140ft of covered space, sufficient for four Swordfish with folded wings.

Tankers, however, were constrained by the need for pipework at the upper deck levels, thus no hangar space was available. The flight decks were, though, significantly longer than those of the grain ships, an extra 40ft or so allowing extra space for ranging Swordfish aft.

Both MAC ship types were fitted with at least four arrester wires. In addition, since the oil ships aircraft were permanently on deck they had the extra protection of side wind checks and a palisade to provide some shelter for their Swordfish.

LEFT Swordfish of 836 NAS on the snow-covered flight deck of the merchant aircraft carrier HMS *Ancylus* in February 1944. Note the engine covers on the aircraft. *Ancylus* and her 'Rapana' class of MAC ships were all oil tanker conversions. Their deck configuration would not permit a hangar to be installed. Consequently their aircraft were permanently ranged on deck, protected only by raising palisade-like wind breaks along the sides of the flight deck. *(FAA Museum)*

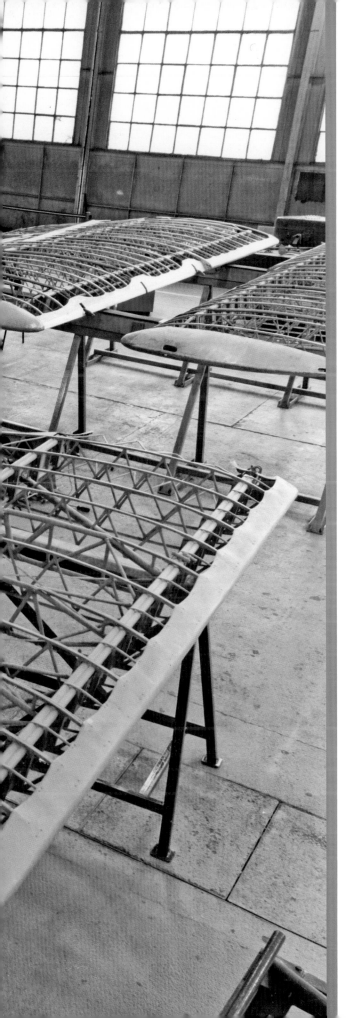

Chapter Three

Swordfish anatomy

The expression 'tried and tested' sums up the way the Swordfish was built. Those who flew her or maintained her can vouch for the toughness of her construction, the simplicity of her systems and the comparative ease with which her structure and systems could be accessed, serviced and repaired in the hangar and at sea.

OPPOSITE The restoration of the RNHF's Swordfish Mark I, W5856, taking place at BAe's Brough factory in the early 1990s. *(BAE Systems)*
(All photos by Jonathan Falconer except where credited)

Introduction

In many respects the construction of the Swordfish was similar to its near contemporary, the Hawker Hurricane, itself a design that evolved from distinguished biplane ancestry. Both aircraft could be considered to reflect a period of transition, when airframes were of composite design. For instance, their part fabric-covered part metal-skinned fuselages formed over tubular metal framing represented a kind of halfway house from the wood and fabric fuselages of the First World War to the all-metal monocoque of the Supermarine Spitfire.

Fuselage

This takes the form of a tubular box, constructed of solid drawn steel tubing. The box is formed with four longerons running fore and aft at each corner; each of the twelve bays in the box is strut-braced bottom and sides, 'W'-fashion like a Warren Girder, with additional strengthening in the form of diagonal tension wires within the box frame. The majority of struts and all the longerons are plug-ended. Connections are provided from the fuselage to the front and rear spars of the stub planes of the lower wing.

A projecting catapult spool is provided on each side of the fuselage, located at lower longeron level, below the rear gun position.

The fuselage is assembled in five parts, known as the engine mounting, the front portion, the centre portion, the rear portion and the rear wedge. Each part or portion is bolted to the next one so as to form a complete fuselage.

Where it is necessary to aid connection of tubing, tubes are distorted into a flat section.

There is a minimum of welding in the aeroplane's structure generally. Fuselage framing sections in particular are connected via flat fish plates, riveted to each member using special thick walled rivets. These are of steel

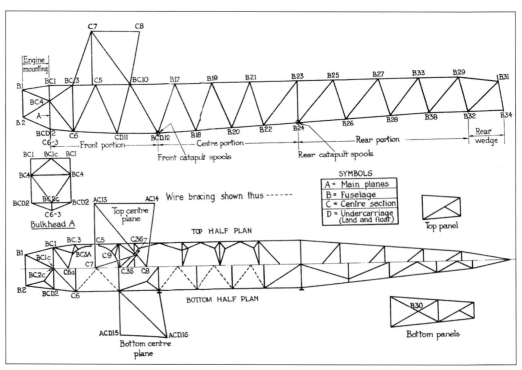

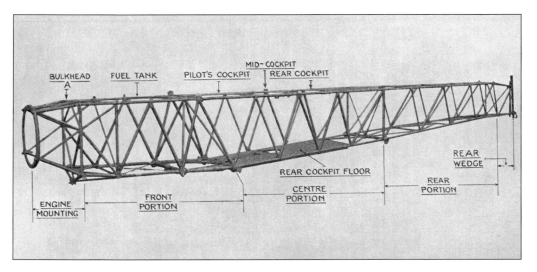

LEFT This perspective view of the fuselage framing demonstrates the way it is assembled from five sections – engine mounting, front portion, centre portion, rear portion and rear wedge. *(AP1517/ RNHF)*

to BSS T 50 and are secured by means of a special conical punch.

All steel tubing forming the fuselage is given anti-corrosion treatment, while light alloy components undergo an anodic process. Cadmium plating of steel is followed up by a coating of tung oil varnish. This serves to confirm that the cadmium or anodic surfaces underneath it are undisturbed and without corrosion.

Numerous attachment points are provided along the fuselage framing. Two examples are shown in the adjoining photographs.

Generally fuselage coverings are of alloy or fabric on wood. A major part of the fuselage

LEFT With the rearmost panel removed the braced nature of the fuselage is clearly visible. Note the V-shaped cross-bracing along the underside of the fuselage.

and the whole area of the engine assembly is made to be accessible by means of detachable panels.

ABOVE This wing attachment point incorporates the spool for catapult launches.

LEFT AND BELOW Swordfish were built to be readily convertible to floatplane form. Little alteration to the landplane configuration was necessary. Twin floats were attached utilising the existing landplane undercarriage geometry. This attachment point (shown in top centre of the upper photo) was one of the few extra provisions that were necessary to effect the change from wheels to floats.

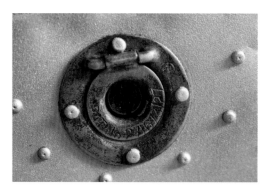

RIGHT Patent Fairey Fastener. This key-type fastener attaches alloy and wood/fabric panels to fuselage framing.

FAR RIGHT Shorn of engine and wings, the fuselage clearly demonstrates the almost total accessibility of the interior of the fuselage forward of the cockpit area by means of the alloy panels.

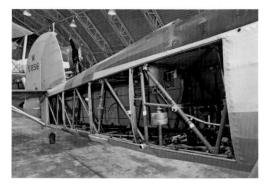

RIGHT Elevator and rudder control cables are shown emerging from the fuselage. Control is effected in both cases by twin cables running on pulleys within the fuselage, connected at one end, in the pilot's cockpit to rudder bars and control column and at the other, via fairleads to kingpost levers mounted on the rudder and elevator.

ABOVE Correct trim is achieved by attaching weights to the vertical spigot shown here. This is fixed within a strengthened section of the fuselage's vertical V-bracing.

Detachable metal and fabric covered wooden panels are secured at fixing points on the fuselage framing by Patent Fairey Fasteners

Provision is made in the rearward fuselage panels for the emergence of empennage flying controls cables with faired exit points built into the respective panels.

Provision is made for trimming the aircraft in the fuselage. Two red-painted projections serve as trimming points to support the datum device. Trim is then achieved by means of circular weights added to a spigot mounting each side of the rear fuselage. Clear panels enable the weights to be checked without the need for panel removal.

RIGHT A closer view of the trim weights.

Central upper plane supports (cabane struts)

The tubular framing in the upper fuselage is extended upwards from the upper longerons in the centre bay of front portion so as to form the framework supporting the top centre plane of the wing. This plane (or cabane) is extended

RIGHT Skeleton of bottom stub plane. Note the robust rib and tube construction. This attaches to the fuselage, is stiffened by the faired V-bracing and provides the attachment points for the lower folding main-planes. *(AP1517/RNHF)*

outwards each side to the point at which the complete wing is folded.

Further bays are extended outwards from the fuselage in similar fashion from the lower longerons each side of the fuselage, so as to provide the framing for bottom stub planes of the wing.

Fuselage covering

Characteristically, practically the whole of the interior of the fuselage can be accessed from the sides for maintenance purposes. This is made possible by means of detachable panels.

These are of aluminium alloy from immediately behind the engine cowling to a point just behind the rear cockpit; from this point rearward there are detachable panels of fabric-covered ply, given a slight camber by wooden formers. These panels give quick access to the interior of the fuselage and its items of equipment, such as the flotation bag.

The underside of the rear fuselage is similarly equipped for access with three detachable aluminium panels attached by Fairey Fasteners. The foremost of these panels has a V-shaped recess to accommodate the frame of the deck arrester gear. This panel extends just beyond the snap release gear for which it provides two housings. The next panel extends from the snap gear to the tail-wheel oleo leg and the final panel covers the underside of the fuselage wedge.

Parts of both centre and rear fuselage portions are covered with fabric, which is laced to the eyeleted edges of metal sheet fixed to formers that bridge the fuselage members. The contours of fabric-covered portions of the fuselage are longitudinally maintained by longeron stringers.

Both metal and wooden panels are shaped to affix to tubular framing. They are provided around their edges with Patent Fairey Fasteners, which engage with a series of catches that are welded to vertical and horizontal tube members.

Two lugs project from the fuselage. Normally painted red these datum points enable the correct C of G to be obtained, using weights at the ballast point in the lower fuselage. This has provision for the addition or deletion of circular weights as required with the ballast state visible at all times through a transparent panel in the fuselage side.

Deck arrester gear

The deck arresting hook is attached to the end of a V-frame, which swings on a cross tube in the fuselage. It drops when released from its snap fitting and is activated and retracted through cable control from the pilot's position in the cockpit.

Details of the cockpit and rear aircrew positions are included on pages 76 to 79.

Bomb-aiming position

Like an RAF contemporary the Westland Lysander, the Swordfish was provided with a prone bomb-aiming position. This was located under the pilot's cockpit and enabled the observer to assist the pilot by aiming bombs and other ordnance. A sliding section with a glazed panel allowed access to the weapon where it was slung beneath the fuselage. In addition clear panels are provided in the

LEFT Arrester gear housing viewed from inside the fuselage.The V-frame of the arrester gear is fully retractable and is housed when retracted within the metal channels. These are seen from above in this view, looking from inside the fuselage towards its underside.

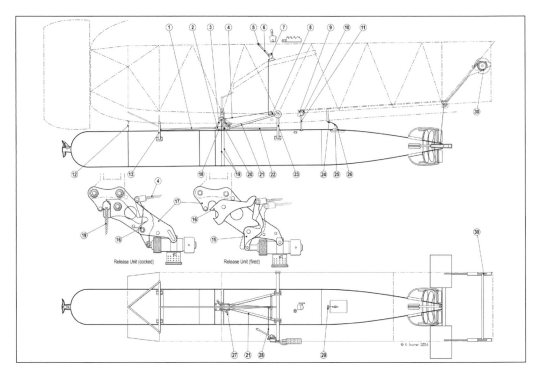

fuselage sides to assist vision during the bomb-aiming function.

Engine mounting

The engine mounting is formed of a tubular framework consisting of four projecting pyramids attached to the forward fuselage at twelve points, to which is fixed an independently detachable flanged metal ring. Due to the handed configuration of the mounting, none of the four pyramids is interchangeable.

High-tensile steel bolts attach the pyramidal structure at its rear to the front tubular bulkhead at top, middle and bottom positions.

The flanged engine mounting ring is attached to the pyramidal framing by four flanged nuts. These engage with the threaded ends of forgings located at the extremities of the pyramidal support. The Bristol Pegasus engine is secured through the face of this ring by eighteen bolts.

Undercarriage

Otherwise known as the alighting gear, this is of the fixed non-retracting type and is divided to enable stores such as a torpedo, mine or bomb to be carried and dropped from its position beneath the fuselage.

Each unit is V-shaped and consists of three elements (or legs) attached to the lower part of the aircraft. The leg known as the axle tube carries a stub axle at its lowest extremity. This leg is positioned by a further leg known as the radius rod, which forms the V-shape below the fuselage. The third element referred to as the oleo leg, acts as the suspension unit and forms a further inverted triangulation with the axle tube and the radius rod.

During service on smaller carriers in the Second World War some Swordfish were modified by arranging wires between the split undercarriage legs. This provision limited the possibility of splay and even collapse, caused when a machine met a rising deck while landing.

Axle tube

This is formed of nickel-chrome steel tubing. The tube is attached to the fuselage framing at its upper end by means of a forked plug bolted to a lug projecting from the lower fuselage longeron. The lower end of the tube is reinforced by a steel tube and in this form passes over the inner end of the tubular stub axle. Two pairs of lugs provide attachment points for fittings for each of the lower ends of the oleo leg and radius rod.

Each of the three undercarriage/landing gear members is provided with an oval section fabric-covered wooden fairing.

The axle tube fairing incorporates the pneumatic pipeline for the braking system. In addition the tube includes a tubular steel crew step at its upper end and a jacking foot on its inner lower face.

Radius rod

Similar in form to the axle tube. Also of nickel-chrome tubing, this leg attaches to the lower fuselage longeron forward of the axle tube. Like the latter element it connects to the fuselage by means of a forked plug, bolted to the longeron lug with a locked nut and split pin. The bolt

incorporates a grease nipple. The rod attaches to the lugged sleeve on the axle tube by means of a forked socket. A tubular steel crew step is provided at the upper tapered end of the rod.

Oleo leg

This third element of the land undercarriage, which completes its triangulation, has the important function of absorbing the loads imposed by the weight of the aircraft when landing. For this purpose it comprises two

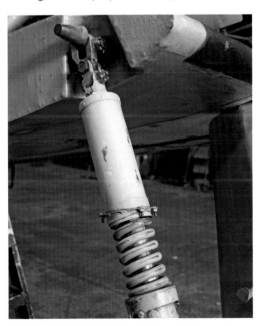

LEFT General view of undercarriage showing oleo, axle and radius struts. This head-on view demonstrates the way in which the undercarriage is effectively a series of triangulations with the triangle of axle and radius struts further triangulated through the oleo leg and with this, in its turn, supported by a stub wing which is itself braced by triangular strutting to the fuselage side.

LEFT Attachment of undercarriage leg to stub wing root. This fitting serves the dual purpose of a) providing an anchorage for the upper end of the oleo leg and b) projecting a locating pin on to which the lower main-plane will be folded.

LEFT Oleo fairing removed. A view from the port side of the lower mainplane stub wing root showing the oleo leg anchorage and locking/locating pin for wing folding. With the oleo leg fairing removed, the combination of telescopic plunger and spring is clearly visible.

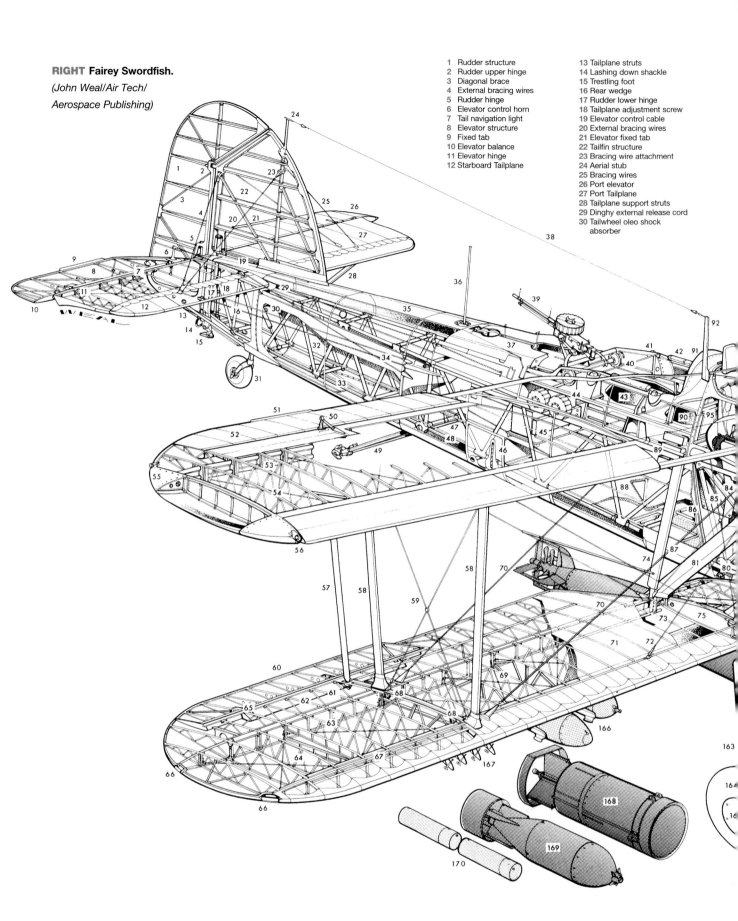

RIGHT Fairey Swordfish.

*(John Weal/Air Tech/
Aerospace Publishing)*

1 Rudder structure
2 Rudder upper hinge
3 Diagonal brace
4 External bracing wires
5 Rudder hinge
6 Elevator control horn
7 Tail navigation light
8 Elevator structure
9 Fixed tab
10 Elevator balance
11 Elevator hinge
12 Starboard Tailplane
13 Tailplane struts
14 Lashing down shackle
15 Trestling foot
16 Rear wedge
17 Rudder lower hinge
18 Tailplane adjustment screw
19 Elevator control cable
20 External bracing wires
21 Elevator fixed tab
22 Tailfin structure
23 Bracing wire attachment
24 Aerial stub
25 Bracing wires
26 Port elevator
27 Port Tailplane
28 Tailplane support struts
29 Dinghy external release cord
30 Tailwheel oleo shock
    absorber

31 Non-retractable Dunlop tailwheel
32 Fuselage framework
33 Arrester hook housing
34 Control cable fairleads
35 Dorsal decking
36 Rod aerial
37 Lewis gun stowage trough
38 Aerial
39 Flexible 0.303-in (7.7-mm) Lewis machine gun
40 Fairey high-speed flexible gun mounting
41 Type O-3 compass mounting points

42 Aft cockpit coaming
43 Aft cockpit
44 Lewis drum magazine stowage
45 Radio installation
46 Ballast weights
47 Arrester hook pivot
48 Fuselage lower longeron
49 Arrester hook (part extended)
50 Aileron hinge

51 Fixed tab
52 Starboard upper aileron
53 Rear spar
54 Wing ribs
55 Starboard formation light
56 Starboard navigation light
57 Aileron connect strut
58 Interplane struts
59 Bracing wires

60 Starboard lower aileron
61 Aileron hinge
62 Aileron balance
63 Rear spar
64 Wing ribs
65 Aileron outer hinge
66 Deck-handling/lashing grips
67 Front spar
68 Interplane strut attachments

69 Wing internal diagonal bracing wires
70 Flying wires
71 Wing skinning
72 Additional support wire (fitted when underwing stores carried)
73 Wing fold hinge
74 Inboard interplane struts
75 Stub plane end rib
76 Wing locking handle
77 Stub plane structure
78 Intake slot
79 Side window
80 Catapult spool
81 Drag struts
82 Cockpit sloping floor
83 Fixed 0.303-in (7.7-mm) Vickers gun (deleted from some aircraft)
84 Case ejection chute
85 Access panel
86 Camera mounting bracket
87 Sliding bomb-aiming hatch
88 Zip inspection flap
89 Fuselage upper longeron
90 Centre cockpit
91 Inter-cockpit fairing
92 Upper wing aerial mast
93 Pilot's headrest
94 Pilot's seat and harness
95 Bulkhead

96 Vickers gun fairing
97 Fuel gravity tank (12.5 Imp gal/57 litre capacity)
98 Windscreen
99 Handholds
100 Flap control handwheel and rocking head assembly
101 Wing centre section
102 Dinghy release cord handle
103 Identification light
104 Centre section pyramid strut attachment
105 Diagonal strengtheners
106 Dinghy inflation cylinder
107 Type C dinghy stowage well
108 Aileron control linkage
109 Trailing edge rib sections
110 Rear spar
111 Wing rib stations
112 Aileron connect strut
113 Port upper aileron
114 Fixed tab
115 Aileron hinge
116 Port formation light
117 Wing skinning
118 Port navigation light
119 Leading-edge slot
120 Front spar
121 Nose ribs
122 Interplane struts
123 Pitot head
124 Bracing wires
125 Flying wires
126 Port lower mainplane
127 Landing lamp
128 Underwing bomb shackles
129 Underwing strengthening plate
130 Rocket-launching rails
131 Four 60-lb (27-g) anti-shipping rocket projectiles
132 Three-blade fixed-pitch Fairey-Reed metal propeller
133 Spinner
134 Townend ring
135 Bristol Pegasus IIIM3 (or Mk 30) radial engine
136 Cowling clips
137 Engine mounting ring
138 Engine support bearers
139 Firewall bulkhead
140 Engine controls
141 Oil tank immersion heater socket
142 Filler cap
143 Oil tank (13.75 Imp gal/62.5 litre capacity)
144 Centre section pyramid struts
145 External torpedo sight bars
146 Fuel filler cap
147 Main fuel tank (155 Imp gal/705 litre capacity)
148 Vickers gun trough
149 Fuselage forward frame
150 Oil cooler
151 Fuel filter
152 Stub plane/fuselage attachment
153 Fuel feed lines
154 Dinghy immersion switch
155 Exhaust
156 Port Dunlop mainwheel
157 Jacking foot
158 1,610-lb (730-kg) 18-in (45.7-cm) torpedo

159 Access/servicing footholds
160 Torpedo forward crutch
161 Radius rod fairing
162 Undercarriage axle tube fairing
163 Undercarriage oleo leg fairing
164 Starboard mainwheel
165 Hub cover
166 Underwing bombs
167 Underwing outboard shackles
168 Depth-charge
169 250-lb (113-kg) bomb
170 Anti-shipping flares

RIGHT An important reminder to maintainers that the oil in the unit must be kept topped up to the required level.

FAR RIGHT The Swordfish was fitted with Dunlop AH 420 wheels with tyres inflated to a pressure of 45psi. The step at the top of the forward undercarriage leg is one of three fitted to enable groundcrew to operate the revolving starter mechanism housed in the fuselage side.

RIGHT To reduce the effects of one-sided wear, tyres are reversed at regular intervals.

tubular steel sections that telescope together as a shock absorber. The outer tube (ie, the lowermost of the two) attaches to a lug on the axle tube while the inner one, the uppermost of the two, is attached to the stub plane by means of a forked plug secured by a bolt, nut and split pin. The shock-absorbing unit contains a combination of springs, plungers and valves.

While in flight the leg is fully extended by its two main springs. On touch-down, compression forces on the leg activate the flow of oil upwards within the unit, under pressure. This takes place in a progressive way so that the shock is initially cushioned, then resisted. A final third rebound phase occurs whereby the main spring flexes and the leg moves downwards again.

Wheels

These are of the Dunlop type, originally pattern AH 420, and are fitted with tyres inflated to a pressure of 45lb/sq in. A grease nipple located on each hub allows the roller bearings of the wheel to be lubricated.

While in service the outer treads of each tyre wear quicker than the inner sections. This tendency is reduced by periodic reversal of each tyre.

Brakes

Braking is effected by means of air pressure supplied from a compressed air container. The

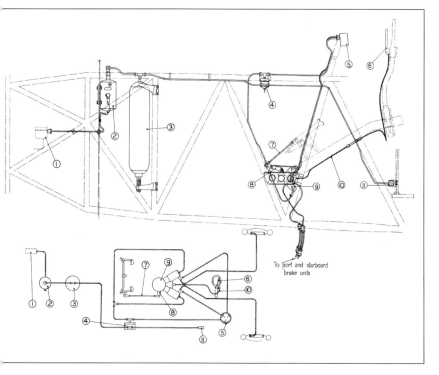

To port and starboard brake units

LEFT Diagrammatic arrangement of wheel brake system. The wheel brake system makes provision for turning when taxying by the actuation of brakes differentially through foot pressure on the appropriate rudder pedal. *(Roy Scorer)*

FAR LEFT AND LEFT
Rear face of main wheel showing brake assembly. The hub area is covered by a curved alloy fairing attached to a light framework by means of Patent Fairey Fasteners. A grease nipple is provided for the lubrication of wheel bearings.

LEFT Brake control valve.

supply of compressed air in the container is maintained by an engine-driven compressor.

The compressed air container takes the form of a cylinder or bottle, retained in hemispherical end caps and bracketed to a strut situated behind the fire bulkhead on the port side of the fuselage front section. Air is forced into the container through a system of valves and stored under pressure until use and replenishment.

When brakes are actuated, air pressure is directed to the brake differential valve from whence it is supplied differentially, as directed by movement of the rudder pedals in the pilot's cockpit.

A triple indicator gauge on the pilot's instrument panel registers brake pressure. With the hand lever at 'ON' this should be 80lb/sq in.

The lever that activates the braking is attached to the neck of the spade grip control column. A Bowden cable connects the lever with the brake differential valve and this is linked back to the pilot's rudder bar so as to effect differential braking for steering purposes when taxying on the ground.

Each wheel is served by a separate pipeline located within the axle tube. The pipeline comprises a combination of copper and flexible tubing. The latter is employed in the vicinity of the flexible joints of the undercarriage. Air reservoirs are built into the lower centre section V-bracing struts.

Provision is made for the replenishment of compressed air from an external source. A Schrader valve projects from the fuselage and is incorporated in a coupling suitable for a standard pump-type compressor.

Tail wheel

The tail wheel is of the Dunlop AHO 5023 type and is kept inflated at a pressure of 55lb/sq in. The wheel is held in a forked leg located at the extremity of the rear fuselage portion where this attaches to the wedge section. The axle which is of hollow steel is held in the fork by its spool shape at one end. At the other threaded end it is locked to the wheel fork by a tab-washered nut.

Like the main units the suspension is of the oleo type incorporating a spring and piston assembly. Oil flows through a valve and piston and is compressed by landing shock

LEFT Tail wheel, general view.

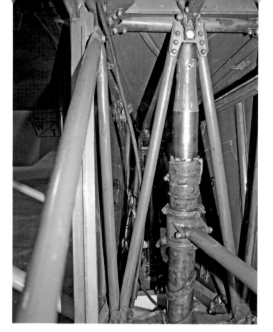

RIGHT Tail-wheel mounting internal view showing the strut of which the tail-wheel oleo post is an extension.

and rebound. However, while stationary, on the ground the rear of the aircraft is wholly supported by the spring component.

The tail assembly incorporates a device whereby the wheel is maintained in line with the fuselage during flight. This is actuated by a cam-shaped collar, which disengages when the aircraft is on the ground enabling the unit to caster freely.

Empennage

mpennage is the term used to describe flying surfaces at the rear of the fuselage. It is comprised of two main elements: the fin and rudder assembly for vertical stabilising and turning, and the tailplane and elevator for stabilising and movement in the horizontal plane. Both elements are constructed of steel and Duralumin and are wholly fabric covered.

Port and starboard sections of the tailplane comprise front and rear spars connected by six drag struts extending rearwards, combined with nose ribs extending forwards within the curved nose-plating at the leading edge, to which they are clipped.

LEFT Empennage showing fin/rudder and tailplane/elevator assemblies including the control cables leading back to the rudder and elevator levers.

LEFT Tailplane adjusting gear hand wheel and mounting looking aft. The tailplane incidence can be adjusted from the cockpit as an aid to trim the attitude of the aircraft. *(Roy Scorer)*

BELOW Uncovered sections of empennage area of the fuselage.

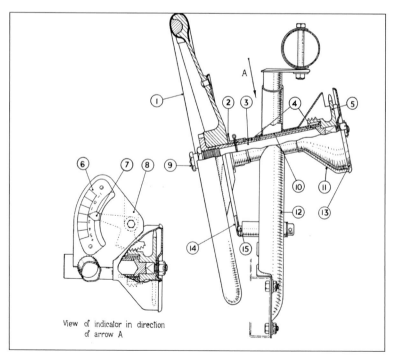

View of indicator in direction of arrow A

The fin is attached to the fuselage by means of front and middle supports on the rear portion and wedge and is secured at the rear to the stern post. It is offset 1 degree 30 minutes to starboard so as to counteract the effect of the slipstream. The rudder, which is horn balanced, is hung on three hinges with plain bearings, two on the stern post and one on the rear fin post.

The tailplane is attached to the fuselage over the rear wedge and is adjustable from the cockpit through a screw mechanism within the fuselage wedge section. The split elevators of the Frise type are hinged to the rear spar of the tailplane and are connected by a central tube. They are horn balanced.

Manual trimming is effected by means of fixed light metal tabs attached to the trailing edges of both elevators and rudder.

The fin and rudder are made up of horizontal ribs and vertical tube, with diagonal bracing. The shape of fin and rudder is formed by curved tube, with the rudder assembly attached at the rear of the fin by three hinges on the fin post and one on the stern post.

The tailplane (or horizontal stabiliser) is supported on each side of the fin by two V-shaped steel bracing wires. These are attached at a single point along the front spar and are fixed to two vertical members within the framework of the fin.

Further support underneath the tailplane is provided each side by two faired tubular metal struts. These are anchored to the fuselage framing at their bases and fixed to tail spars at their upper ends.

A tubular hinge connects both port and starboard elevators. This passes through a slot in the rudder and is cranked to allow full elevator movement. The slot is incorporated in a fairing and is balsa-wood lined.

A fairing located at the penultimate horizontal rib includes a mounting bracket to which is fixed the tail navigation light.

A foldaway V-strut is hinged to the undersides of the tailplane each side of the fuselage. When in use these attach to the lower mainplanes so as to retain them in the folded position.

A stub aerial post is located on the

upper leading edge of the fin with an aerial cable running from this point to a short mast mounted above the pilot on the upper mainplane. When in service an additional aerial rod was located on the coaming immediately behind the retractable machine gun housing with a navigation light located at the lower trailing edge of the rudder.

When fitted radio equipment is located immediately rearwards of the TAG position.

A dinghy release cable projects from the top of the fuselage near the base of the fin/rudder assembly.

The outer frame of the rudder comprises a curved trailing edge tube, a tubular post and a diagonal rib of channel section of Duralumin.

The rudder is stiffened by eight horizontal ribs which are riveted to the outer frame members by flanged spool attachments at front and rear ends.

Projecting from the fuselage adjacent to the line of the rudder hinge are two features, a lashing-down shackle and a trestling foot, used when lifting the rear of the aircraft.

ABOVE Trim tabs are attached to the trailing edges of the rudder and elevator control surfaces. They are manually adjustable to give appropriate trim correction.

LEFT Underside of tail/elevator. Note the twin struts supporting the tailplane from the lower fuselage side. Also the V-shaped tubular frame which, when deployed forward, retains the wings of the Swordfish in the folded position. When not in use this is retracted and held up to the underside of the tailplane by a snap catch.

ABOVE The top wing centre section of the upper mainplane, when covered and fitted, forms the cabane part of the top wing. Its framing is formed of standard ribs and riblets held within a cross-braced tubular frame. *(AP1517 /RNHF)*

Wings

The wing configuration is that of a two-bay biplane with mainplanes of unequal span, the straight lower wing being shorter than the upper one. In addition, the upper mainplane has a 4-degree sweepback, thus ensuring the correct C of G.

Ailerons are provided on all four mainplanes. The upper port and starboard ailerons are cable operated via external levers. The lower port and starboard pair are linked to those in the upper mainplane by faired interconnecting struts.

The design of the Swordfish reflects its multi (TBR) roles. To this end the aircraft were provided with dual purpose flap/airbrake facilities.

While rarely used in action in a true dive-bombing attitude, should this need arise the turning of a knurled knob, centrally placed, above the pilot's head, on the trailing edge of the upper centre mainplane, effectively 'converted' ailerons to dive brakes.

In practice, the flying qualities of the Swordfish were such that less use was made of the conventional flap arrangement than was the case in other similar aircraft types.

To facilitate hangar stowage and so as to fit lift dimensions on carriers, the wings of the

RIGHT The flap control wheel and rocking head assembly is located above the pilot's head. When turned it converts the differential aileron movement to one where both control surfaces move together, thereby providing a flap or dive-brake facility for the pilot.

RIGHT Rocking head assembly moved to left.

RIGHT Calibration lines on aileron to flap control torque tube.

RIGHT Folding the wings of a Swordfish reduces its overall width from 45ft 6in (13.88m) to 17ft 3in (5.25m). These dimensions apply in both landplane and the floatplane versions.

Swordfish fold back along the fuselage. In this form the width of the aircraft is reduced from 45ft 6in to 17ft 3in, or a little over one-third of its span when the wings are spread.

To put this dimension in context, Fleet and Escort Carrier maximum flight deck width was of the order of 80ft to 95ft, while that of MAC ships rarely exceeded 60ft.

Wing-locking mechanism

Each mainplane assembly pivots on a rear bracket and locks on to the forward equivalent.

The locking mechanism is clearly marked in red and comprises a steel lock pin housed in the innermost forward interplane strut. This is locked by downward movement of a curved

ABOVE Wing stub showing attachment points and undercarriage. Note the alignment of the oleo leg and the inverted V-strutting. This juxtaposition ensures upward forces from the undercarriage on the stub wing are resisted by the strutting.

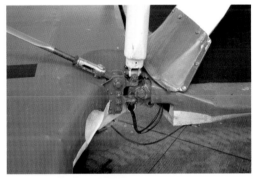

LEFT Rear bracket. The port mainplane assembly hinges at this point when wing folding takes place. Note the fairing at the base of the V-strut and the streamlined section of the interplane bracing wire.

LEFT Forward bracket shown with the wing folded and the locking mechanism in the open position.

FAR LEFT Lock pin. This is cone-shaped to locate in an aperture in the outer lower mainplane. It is also slotted vertically so as to receive the retractable bolt which is incorporated in the locking mechanism housed on the inner forward interplane strut of the outer mainplane.

pressed steel handle. The pin penetrates a slot in the conical alignment pin attached to both top and bottom stub planes, port and starboard. The actuating handle is painted red and is clearly visible in daylight. As a further precaution, the locking mechanism can be secured in place by a circular pin inserted through the pin from the side of the strut.

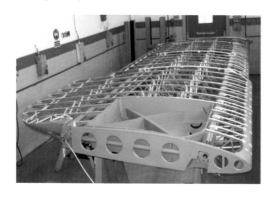

Wing construction

There are seven separate elements; port and starboard upper and lower mainplanes, port and starboard stub wings and the top centre plane above the pilot's position. The first four elements fold, the remaining three are fixed to the fuselage.

The construction of all seven elements is similar, being based on front and rear spars, with leading and central ribs, trailing ribs stiffened by diagonally arranged bracing wires.

Taking the lower mainplane as an example, this comprises 14 standard ribs with 2 end ribs stiffened by 4 girder ribs, a drag rib and a drag strut. Bays, apart from the innermost one, are all diagonally cross braced by streamlined wires.

Spars are of built-up steel, comprised of upper and lower tubular booms. These are rolled to a circular section and act as flanges

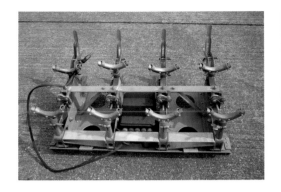

of a beam. They are provided with a flange for riveted attachment to the spar web, which is stiffened by riveted stabilising plates each side.

Apart from under-wing metal sheathing to mainplanes provided on Swordfish Mark II, all wing surfaces are fabric covered using Irish linen. Once covered the wings are treated with several coats of dope, rubbed down between each application and finished with camouflage colours and insignia as appropriate.

Each upper mainplane wingtip displays a navigation light at the leading edge and a formation light at the trailing edge.

Bomb carriers

To facilitate the carrying of stores three eyebolts are inserted vertically through the lower booms of each of three girder ribs. As a strengthening measure each of these has transverse diagonal bracing linking the rib to the rear spar. A further two ribs outboard of the main stores attachment points are fitted with lugs to their lower booms. These are able to support light bombs.

Weapons loads were often of a composite nature, as required by the nature of the mission. For example, while inner bomb carriers were stressed to carry heavy stores such as 3 x 250lb HE or SAP ordnance under each wing, the light load carriers would be used to carry smoke floats, flares or other marking devices, or light bombs where less extensive or softer-skinned targets were involved. Bomb release was effected through the withdrawal of a claw or hook, actuated by an electric solenoid and operated by the pilot's firing button in the front cockpit.

External rigging

Upper and lower mainplanes are joined by two pairs of streamlined section interplane struts. These are of metal, faired with fabric over a

SWORDFISH BITE – ARMAMENT

Guns	1 × fixed, forward-firing .303in Vickers machine gun in starboard engine cowling.
	1 × trainable .303in Vickers K or Lewis machine gun in rear cockpit.
Rockets	8 × 3in 60lb RP-3 rocket projectiles on under-wing racks (Swordfish Mark II and later).
Air-dropped weapons	1 × 18in Mark XII 1,610lb torpedo or A Mark I–IV 1,500lb mine under fuselage or 6 x 250lb bombs or 6 x 250lb depth charges under fuselage and wings.
	4½in reconnaissance flares.

steamlined profile. Bases of the struts are faired onto the wing surface to reduce drag.

The pitot tube, which feeds pressure readings to the airspeed indicator is located on the upper part of the forward port interplane strut.

The struts in their turn, are braced by stainless steel incidence wires, fitted between each top and bottom plane. Further, the bays so formed have lift and anti-lift wires located in line with the front and rear spars.

An additional wire serves to brace each lower mainplane in the area wing in which weapons loads require extra support. This runs from the underside of the centreplane to the front spar just outboard of the inner interplane struts.

Rigging wing assemblies requires accurate adjustment. To this end rigging wires are provided with turnbuckles, akin to a bottle screw, with which to brace mainplanes. Turnbuckles are fitted with locknuts at their ends.

Auto slots or slats

These are mounted along the outer leading edge of each upper mainplane. First introduced by Herr Junkers the German aviation pioneer and subsequently adopted by the British company Handley Page these are an anti-stall device which delay the break-up of airflow over the leading edge of wings as speed decreases.

In the case of the Swordfish they extend outwards to the wingtips of the port and starboard mainplanes. The slats are formed of 24swg. Duralumin is welded end to end, with internal formers to give a curved contour. Each of these is attached to the mainplane by three track bars which are bolted to front underside of the slat. The track bars are located and run between upper and lower rotating roller guides.

Ailerons

Generally top and bottom ailerons are constructed along similar lines to the mainplanes. Rib webs are, however, of stamped Duralumin with flanged lightening holes. The aileron hinge mechanism takes the form of rearward extensions of mainplane ribs which project beneath the under-surface of the mainplane.

Top and bottom ailerons operate together by means of interconnecting struts which are incorporated in the outer portion of the intermediate hinge.

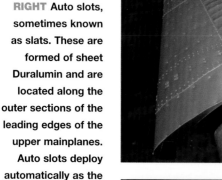

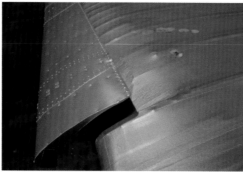

The ailerons are actuated by a vertical arm which connects by push-pull rod through a hole in the spar web to a double armed pivotal lever, working on a bracket fixed to the front face of the rear spar.

Wingtip handles

Wingtips are cut away along the trailing edge to provide a grip for handling crew when aircraft are taxying in windy conditions or require manhandling in the course of being ranged on flight decks.

Landing lamp

The G-type landing light is housed in a bay between two ribs, attached by flanged channels to the front spar web. The push-pull control for the lamp is led through a bracket supported by a transverse channel attached at each end to the lower booms of the two adjoining ribs.

Cables for bombs flare and landing light run in conduit through a hole in the rear end of the bottom mainplane root. Bomb cables run transversely through the mainplane eventually terminating in sockets on the lower boom sections of appropriate ribs.

Front inner interplane struts

As already indicated these struts perform an important role in that they accommodate the mainplane locking mechanisms. The struts are of steel tube faired to a streamlined shape by aluminium leading edges with tapered wooden formers behind.

Flying controls

Flying control surfaces are operated through a combination of cable and rod connections. Ailerons and elevators are operated through movement of the control column. Floor pedals control movement of the rudder.

Taking rudder controls first, these are actuated by 15cwt cables connected to the floor-mounted rudder bar. The cables are led rearward via grooved pulleys to emerge at a point behind the rear cockpit. Clips are used to separate the cables and prevent chafing in the slipstream. The cables are attached to the rudder levers through eye

LEFT Aileron interconnecting struts. These transfer movement from the upper to the lower set of ailerons.

LEFT Wingtip handle used by deck handlers/groundcrew as a steadying device, especially when taxying. Note the lashing-down point incorporated in the same wingtip position.

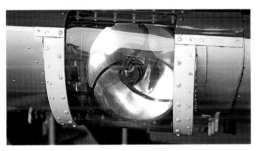

LEFT Landing lamp. This is an adjustable fitting and is located in a housing that projects forward from the leading edge of the port lower mainplane.

LEFT Rudder bar assembly and pilot's floor. Note the raised pilot's floor which allows the observer to take up a prone bomb-aiming position. *(AP1517/RNHF)*

ABOVE Pilot's cockpit and instrument panel, general view. The weapon firing button is located at 11 o'clock on the spade grip handle of the control column.

bolts. Tension rod adjusters are fitted to the cables at the rudder end and rearwards of the rudder bar connections.

The cables are doubled up as a safety measure. In addition a torsion bar cranked through a slot in the lower part of the rudder enables both port and starboard elevators to operate together, in the event of a cable failing on either side.

Next, elevator control. This is effected in a similar manner to that of the rudder, with the exception that elevators are operated by movement of the control column; 20cwt cables run from double arm levers at its base to kingpost levers on the elevators, utilising fairleads on the same fuselage frame strut and emerging via a further set at the same position as the rudder control cables. Ball bearings ensure free running of all pulleys.

Aileron controls are principally of the push-pull tube type. Only the top ailerons are actuated directly with movement transmitted to the lower ones by interconnecting struts. A 20cwt cable connects pulleys at the base of the control column with a rocking lever positioned

behind the top centreplane spar. From this point the aileron controls are rod operated.

Cockpits

Provision is made for an aircrew complement of three comprising pilot, observer and telegraphist air gunner (TAG). It should be explained that these designations reflect FAA practice. Such nomenclature has always differed from that of the RAF, while functions have been basically the same. For instance, the Swordfish observer undertook duties very similar to those of the RAF navigator. Again the FAA retained the use of the shipboard term telegraphist for the role of wireless operator.

One important factor to be borne in mind was that the observer would be in overall command of the aircraft and its mission.

Cockpit accommodation reflects the above aircrew functions with respectively front to rear positions for pilot, observer and TAG.

More detailed description and information is given on pages 82 to 84 but in general terms all flying and engine controls are at hand to the pilot in the front cockpit. In particular the most important weapons selection switch is located in the pilot's cockpit although the observer provided assistance when bomb aiming was required.

A rudimentary aiming sight was installed when torpedo operations were being carried out. This consisted of a narrow arm curved on a wide chord, furnished with an array of light bulbs and placed in the pilot's vision and attached ahead of him to the centre section struts. When lit up, this was used to calculate the aiming-off point for an enemy vessel target, based upon factors such as range and vessel speed.

The observer, who has the bomb-aiming function when the aircraft is being used in that role, has a small number of repeater instruments to assist in this task. In addition, for navigation purposes, there are four compass mounts, two each side on the sills of the rear cockpit.

There is provision for rudimentary seats and floor-based safety harnesses for both observer and TAG.

FAR LEFT Pilot's cockpit, port side.

LEFT Pilot's cockpit, starboard side. Prominent on this side is the blue handle of the fuel cock shown upper left.

LEFT Observer's position.

BELOW LEFT
Observer's ASI and altimeter repeaters. These instruments in the rear cockpit, which duplicate those in the pilot's cockpit, provide essential data for the observer tasked with the responsibility of navigating the aircraft.

LEFT Observer's Morse key. The use of wireless transmissions in Morse enabled signals to be sent at long range and with greater security than would have been the case with radio transmissions.

RIGHT TAG position
in LS326. In flight,
the TAG's position is
marginally draughtier
than that of the
observer!

BELOW Annotated drawing of gun position. Known as the Fairey high speed mounting, the mechanism supporting the machine gun permitted the weapon to be brought into action quickly from its retracted position. It was a considerable improvement on its predecessor, the First World War-vintage Scarff ring. *(AP1517/RNHF)*

The TAG occupied the rearmost position in the aircraft. His weapon was normally the Vickers Gas Operated (VGO) .303 machine gun. This was fixed on a Fairey high-speed mounting. This replaced the First World War-vintage Scarff ring. A further sophistication was the retraction of the weapon when not in use, below and flush with the rear fuselage coaming. Four pan-type magazines could be carried, two strapped each side of the rear cockpit.

Provision for the third crew member TAG was dispensed with on occasion. First, where added range was sought and the overload or long-range auxiliary fuel tank was required to be fitted. Since this left no space for the TAG and dispensing with the VGO machine gun and ammunition helped compensate for the extra weight of the tank. Second, the action at Taranto was an early example of this. Subsequently as the role of the Swordfish focussed on anti-shipping and anti-U-boat work, ASV radar equipment operated by the observer took up space and precluded the carrying of a TAG.

Fortuitously Swordfish operations increasingly took place in areas where enemy

LEFT Swordfish TAG and Vickers Gas Operated (VGO) machine gun (note the primitive ring and bead sight). Care had to be exercised by the TAG when firing the weapon since there was no interrupter device preventing him from hitting his own aircraft. *(Copyright unknown)*

fighter activity was limited if not non-existent. Accordingly the use of either fixed and flexible armament was unlikely to be called upon with the fixed forward-firing gun deleted at a quite early stage.

LEFT Gun release mounting detail.

WARNING
DO NOT RELEASE GUN
MOUNTING WITHOUT GUN
IN POSITION AS THE
MOUNTING IS SPRING
LOADED

BELOW The .303in-calibre machine gun is shown in the retracted position.

BELOW TAG on the alert. Note the TAG's left hand steadying the Fairey mounting while taking aim with the VGO machine gun with the observer focussed on taking a compass bearing. *(FAA Museum)*

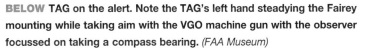

1   Very pistol cartridges
2   Lighting switch panel
3   Mixture control lever
4   Throttle lever (with press-
    to-transmit button)
5   Inertia starter
6   Engine cut-out control
7   Cockpit light dimmer
    switch
8   Boost starters
9   Boost pressure gauge
10 Landing lamp dip control
11 Triple brake pressure
    gauge
12 Ki-Gass priming pump
    button
13 Oil by-pass valve control
14 Rudder pedals (x 2)
15 Altimeter (partially
    obscured by spade grip)
16 Direction indicator
17 Airspeed Indicator
18 Fuel pressure indicator
    light
19 Fuel gauge control switch
20 Compass
21 Control column pilot's
    spade grip
22 Gun firing button
23 Brake control lever
24 Artificial horizon (partially
    obscured by spade grip)
26 Starter switch
27 Cylinder head
    temperature
28 Engine speed indicator
    (rpm)
29 Turn and bank indicator
30 Oil pressure gauge
31 Oil temperature gauge
32 Air suction gauge
33 Cockpit light switch
34 Clock
35 Fuel cock
36 Downward identification
    Morse key
37 De-icer control

PILOT'S COCKPIT EQUIPMENT

Much of the instrumentation together with many of the controls represents the standard equipment of Fleet Air Arm and RAF aircraft of the mid- to late thirties. The spade-type grip of the control column, as well as the fuel controls and instrumentation, are of similar design to their counterparts in the cockpits of the single-seat Supermarine Spitfire and Hawker Hurricane.

Flying controls

These operate control surfaces comprising ailerons, elevators and rudder through a system of levers actuated by cables and pulleys, running from the pilot's position.

The control column controls both the fore, aft and lateral attitude of the aircraft, thus inducing climb, dive and banking movements. The short column is topped with a circular spade grip, the most prominent feature of which is the gun firing button in the 11 o'clock position. This controls the fixed forward-firing Vickers or Browning machine gun when this is fitted.

A spring-loaded brake lever is located behind the spade grip. When squeezed this operates the wheel brakes, either differentially in tune with the rudder when turning, or equally to stop the aircraft when proceeding ahead.

Rudder pedals

These yaw the aircraft in flight, assisting the aileron movement when turning the aircraft, keeping it in balance. When foot pressure is applied, the brake pedals move left or right, depending on which way the pilot wishes to turn. The pedals are operated in conjunction with movement of the control column.

The brakes are operated pneumatically by air pressure supplied to bellows, which then apply brake pressure to each wheel.

The designers of the Swordfish dispensed with elevator trimmers, normally fitted to give slight variations in trim to reduce control forces. Instead, as an alternative, the tailplane and elevator assembly is designed to move with variable incidence. This variable incidence tailplane allows the pilot to remove control forces in level flight once the aircraft has been established at the required speed. The degree of incidence, which varies from 0 to 5 degrees, is controlled by a small wheel similar to a trimmer wheel, located below and to the left of the pilot. As an additional aid, pliable metal strips are attached to the elevator trailing edges.

Engine controls

As already indicated these are the same if not similar to other single-engined military aircraft of the period and follow the convention of having principal engine controls to the left of the pilot's position.

These controls affect the volume and proportions of the fuel/air being fed to the engine, together with the pressure created by the aircraft's supercharger, thus controlling the power produced in any given situation or attitude of the aircraft.

The pilot has no control over the supercharger itself.

The power produced by the engine is measured by the amount that manifold intake pressure exceeds atmospheric pressure. The resultant difference is termed 'boost'.

Throttle and mixture controls

These take the form of two levers, running in a slotted quadrant, below and to the left of the pilot's position. The innermost and larger of the two controls the quantity of fuel being fed to the engine. The smaller outer lever, which has less travel in its own slotted frame, controls the mixture (ie the proportion of air to petrol). This is marked from 'WEAK' to 'RICH'. A button recessed into the top of the throttle handle will initiate radio transmission.

Fuel supply fuel cock

A blue turning handle at the right-hand side of the pilot's seat controls the flow of fuel to the engine from main and header tanks. It is clearly marked 'OFF', 'NORMAL BOTH TANKS', 'GRAVITY ONLY' and 'MAIN ONLY' (see Chapter 7 for details of the operation of these controls).

Fuel gauge

An aperture in the instrument panel at upper right reveals two float gauges, one on the main fuel tank and the other on the header tank. This instrument has its own light, operated by a switch on the instrument panel. The header tank is filled from the main tank by a fuel pump driven off the engine. The engine can be fed with fuel directly from the main tank under fuel pump pressure or from the header tank under gravity. Due to the unreliability of the engine-driven pump it is normal practice to fly the aircraft with 'NORMAL BOTH TANKS' selected. In the event of a fuel pump failure, the pilot can use the 20min of fuel left in the header tank to land, or alternatively he can operate the emergency hand pump to keep the header tank topped up until he can land. A fuel gauge displays the fuel state of the header tank.

Fuel indicator light
This light shows red when fuel pressure falls below a safe level, thus indicating an engine-driven fuel pump failure.

Ki-Gass hand pump
This is a priming device. It is screwed in a clockwise direction and locked down when not in use as per the instructions given on the head (see Chapter 7 for details of its use).

Magneto controls
These switches are on the left-hand side of the instrument panel and control left- and right-hand magnetos and their supply of electric current for the engine ignition system. Since both magnetos are in operation when the engine is running, switching off either magneto will automatically register failing power if the other magneto is faulty.

Boost meter (or gauge)
This is calibrated to measure the increase in pressure supplied by the supercharger as the pilot operates the engine throttle. It is measured at the induction manifold and shows the increase in psi above atmospheric (ie barometric) pressure, eg +2lb boost is recommended for take-off purposes.

Rev counter
The rev counter measures the speed of rotation of the propeller in revolutions per minute (rpm). This is shown on a calibrated dial immediately ahead of the pilot and to the left of the main instrument panel. Pilots are advised of optimum rpm for all flying states.

Slow-running cut-out control
This is located close to the magneto controls and is used to stop the engine in normal operations.

Cockpit light
The cockpit light is operated by a push-pull switch which is located above the clock on the right-hand side of the instrument panel.

FLIGHT INSTRUMENTS
These measure and advise the pilot of a) the in-flight behaviour of the aircraft and b) the state of the various engine and associated control systems.

In-flight behaviour
Five key instruments provide checks for the pilot:

Altimeter
Registers the height of the aircraft above a predefined pressure setting. The calibration of this instrument is based on barometric pressure received at the take-off location. This reading is usually confirmed by radio with airfield control and the instrument's calibration adjusted accordingly. It can be adjusted to give a) height above mean sea level or b) height above the departure/arrival point.

BELOW The altimeter can be seen behind and to the left of the control column.

Airspeed Indicator (ASI)

Operated by air pressure from a pitot head, which registers both dynamic and static pressures. The difference between the two sources gives the dynamic pressure, which is a direct measurement of the aircraft speed. This is displayed to the pilot on the ASI by means of a pointer moving round a scale graduated in knots (ie measuring nautical as distinct from statute mph).

Three instruments are based on a gyroscopic installation. This ensures that they relate to a fixed or 'rigid' plane irrespective of the aircraft's movements.

Direction Indicator

This instrument overcomes the time lag experienced with the aircraft's compass by providing the pilot with an almost instantaneous measurement of turn. This is shown by means of a horizontal, moving semicircular scale graduated in degrees and visible through a small window in the instrument panel.

Turn and Slip Indicator

The balance and rate of turn of the aircraft is shown by this instrument. It is indicated by the movement of a vertical bar relative to top and bottom arcs. The extent of any slip is shown by a simple bubble tube.

Artificial Horizon

This shows the pilot the attitude of the aircraft in relation to the horizon, a necessary requirement when the view from the aircraft is obscured by darkness, fog or cloudy weather. A symbol representing the aircraft will indicate any change in the attitude of the aeroplane by its movement relative to the fixed horizontal bar.

The above three instruments are grouped in a central panel directly ahead of the pilot.

ENGINE INSTRUMENTS

To operate efficiently the engine requires fuel of a specific quantity and at a specific rate. It also needs a consistent flow of lubricant, maintained at an even temperature, which complements airflow over the engine to resist the tendency to overheat as well as lubricating and cooling all moving metal-to-metal surfaces.

The following instruments measure the extent to which these criteria are being met when the aircraft is operating.

Cylinder-head temperature gauge

This is measured by means of a thermocouple thermometer fitted under the sparking plug on top of the cylinder. The thermocouple operates on the principle of the generating of a charge from two dissimilar metals. The resultant impulse is fed to a millivoltmeter with a dial graduated in degrees. This gauge is situated on the pilot's instrument panel.

Fuel pressure indicator

Shows red when fuel pump pressure falls below a safe working level. This may indicate pump failure.

Oil pressure gauge

Operated by oil pressure, which is transmitted via a capillary tube to the instrument. It measures the difference between the pressure of oil in the system and standard atmospheric pressure.

Oil temperature gauge

The measurement of the temperature in the lubricating system is generated by expanding gas and registers on a scale graduated to show changes in degrees C.

EMERGENCY EQUIPMENT

When in operation Swordfish were fitted with an inflatable three-man dinghy and a flotation bag for use in emergencies.

The M Type dinghy is stowed in a compartment in the wing root of the port top plane. It is inflated automatically by an F-type head on the Mark I compressed carbon dioxide cylinder, which is activated electrically by water penetrating the elements of the immersion switch mounted on the forward face of the engine firewall. The cylinder is located in the dinghy stowage. Dinghy manual release is by two cables: one attached to an automatic head and handle on the top centre section; the second is a handle in the centre section leading aft on starboard side of fuselage. Release can be initiated by pulling anywhere along the cable length.

The flotation gear was located in the rear fuselage and comprised an atmospheric airbag.

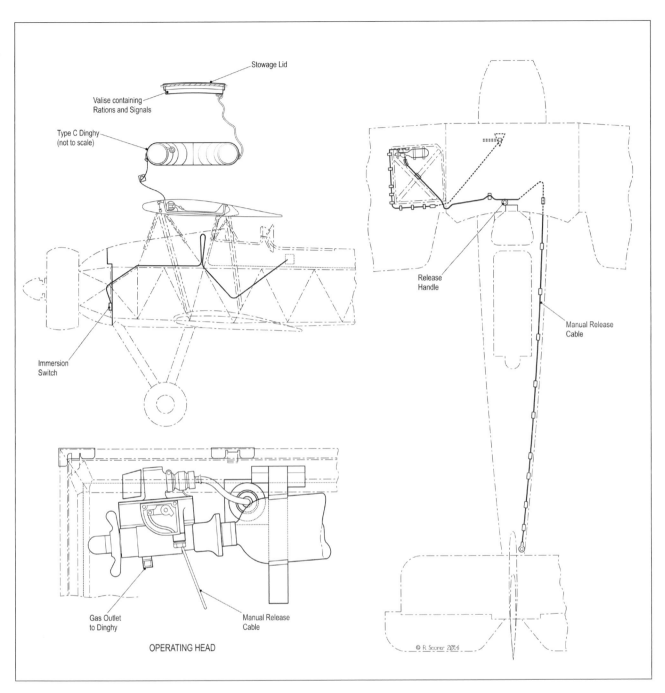

Stowage Lid

Valise containing
Rations and Signals

Type C Dinghy
(not to scale)

Immersion
Switch

Release
Handle

Manual Release
Cable

Gas Outlet
to Dinghy

Manual Release
Cable

OPERATING HEAD

© R. Scorer 2014

ABOVE Diagrammatic illustration of dinghy and associated equipment. Dinghies were prone to inflate without warning while in flight, requiring prompt emergency action in the cockpit. *(Roy Scorer)*

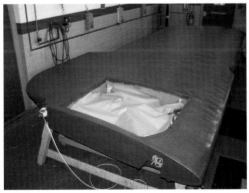

RIGHT Dinghy stowage inside the port wing topplane. This view shows a newly doped mainplane that is yet to receive the cover for the dinghy compartment. *(Copyright unknown)*

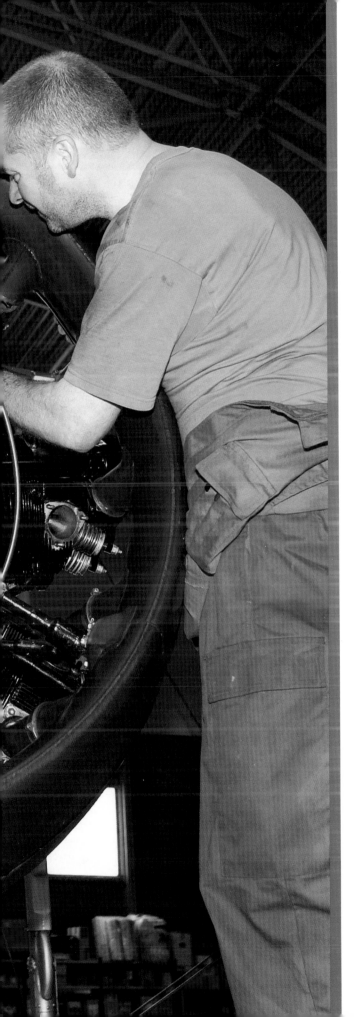

Chapter Four

The Bristol Pegasus engine

‘Faithful Peggy’ as it was sometimes called, the Bristol Pegasus radial engine matched its Swordfish airframe for toughness and dependability. As the engine of choice for many other famous contemporary aircraft, both civil and military, it earned a reputation for reliability that was second to none.

OPPOSITE Maintainer Dave Skiddy works on a Bristol Pegasus engine at the Flight. *(RNHF)*
(All photos by Jonathan Falconer except where credited)

Origins

The Bristol Pegasus nine-cylinder radial engine was a legendary engineering achievement. Known as 'Faithful Peggy' by its many admirers, it was synonymous with toughness and reliability. Introduced in 1932, the engine powered some of the greatest products of the British aircraft industry from the early 1930s onwards. The engine was fitted to both civil and military designs, including the Vickers Wellington and the Short C-class Empire and Sunderland flying boats.

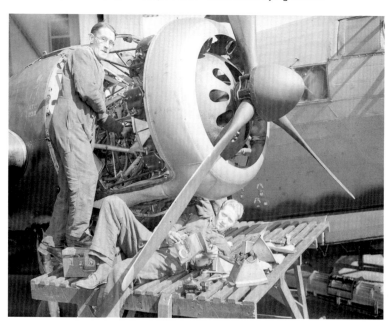

The Pegasus's designer Roy (later Sir Roy) Fedden, who was in charge of engine development at the Bristol Aeroplane Company, had been responsible for the firm's earlier, successful design, the Jupiter. This stemmed from a design evolved by Fedden with a colleague 'Bunny' Butler when working for the Brazil Straker Company as early as 1917. By 1930 the Jupiter had been flown in some 260 different aircraft types, it was the radial engine of choice of Imperial Airways and the RAF and was being licence-built in over a dozen countries.

By taking the Jupiter and reducing the stroke of the pistons from 7½in to 6½in as well as incorporating improvements such as more efficient cooling fins and reducing the weight of the engine's reduction gear, Fedden was able to create a more compact more efficient engine. This was the Mercury. It was a version of this engine, reverting in its design to the longer stroke of the Jupiter, which evolved into the Pegasus, the new name being bestowed at the behest of the Air Ministry, Bristol's principal customer.

The record of the Pegasus was impressive. Licence-built versions came off production lines in Sweden, Czechoslovakia and Poland. It is believed over 40 different types of foreign aircraft were eventually powered by these Pegasus engines. Over 20 foreign air forces used the engine in their military aircraft.

Despite the success of the new engine, production of the short-stroke Mercury continued in parallel as it was found to be eminently suitable for the new fighters and high-performance bombers coming into service. In this connection it is ironic that when Malta's famous Bristol Mercury-powered Sea Gladiators took off to defend the island during the Second World War, they would have been challenging *Regia Aeronautica* Savoia-Marchetti S.M.79 bombers fitted with the stablemate engine of the Pegasus, in this case manufactured under licence by Alfa Romeo.

The Bristol Pegasus and its smaller cousin played a vital role in the expansion of the RAF, especially in the creation of a modern bomber force. Blenheims, Hampdens and Wellingtons with their Mercury and Pegasus powerplants took much of the brunt of the early bombing campaign. Eventually, almost 12,000 of these three RAF medium bombers would be fitted with versions of the Mercury or the Pegasus.

Many other RAF types relied on one or other of the engines, the Short Sunderland and Westland Lysander being just two examples. This fact underlines the wide range of roles and types that took advantage of the engines' qualities.

By the outbreak of war in 1939 later versions of the Pegasus were developing over 1,000hp for a little over the equivalent figure of weight in lbs – a significant achievement, particularly for an engine that had given not much more than half this power at its introduction in the early thirties.

As an outstanding example of radial aero-engine design, the Pegasus represented the outcome of research and development in a fiercely competitive market. That is, in the sense that Bristol was in competition with other British manufacturers of radial engines such as Armstrong Siddeley, but also because a powerful aviation lobby preferred the rival alternative liquid-cooled in-line designs, as exemplified by the famous Rolls-Royce Merlin.

Perhaps most significant of all was the potential for export sales. Here Bristol experienced firm competition from abroad. German, Italian and French engine companies, respectively BMW, Fiat and Gnome Rhône, and strove for the favours of the airframe manufacturers. Across the Atlantic in the US, excellent radial engines such as Pratt and Whitney and Wright designs dominated the market, one which was perhaps less beset by competition from liquid-cooled in-line engines.

Over 17,000 Pegasus engines were eventually produced. More than 14,000 of these came from so-called Shadow Factories involving manufacturers from other sectors of industry such as car and vehicle production, Austin Motors being a typical example.

Building on their achievements with the Pegasus, Roy Fedden and his team at Bristol went on to pioneer the sleeve valve radial engine. The development of this design, though of lengthy duration, culminated in the magnificent twin-row 18-cylinder 2,500hp Bristol Centaurus (this powerplant equips the Royal Navy Historic Flight's Sea Fury aircraft).

Key features of the Pegasus for its time were a good power-to-weight ratio and relatively compact size, especially in its front to back dimension. Other helpful aids to engine performance included deeper fin depth for better cylinder cooling, quick start fuel and oil systems and lighter reduction gearing than hitherto.

Finally, the excellent performance of the Pegasus in record-breaking flights before the Second World War augured well for its use under arduous wartime conditions. In November 1938 two Vickers Wellesleys (powered with the Pegasus) of the RAF Long Range Development Flight established a world record for a nonstop flight of 7,162 miles between Ismailia in Egypt and Darwin in Australia, covered in 48 hours.

When fitted in the Vickers Vespa VII, the Pegasus IS3 helped that aircraft achieve an altitude of just under 44,000ft in September 1932. The record was raised by 10,000ft some five years later in June 1937 when the Bristol 138A monoplane, fitted with a Pegasus PE.6S engine with two-stage supercharger and intercooler, attained a world record height of just under 54,000ft.

Other record-breaking flights enhanced the engine's reputation. The Westland Houston PV3 aircraft used for the first flight over Mount Everest in April 1933 benefited from the Pegasus's reliability, coupled in this case with its high-altitude flight potential.

Taken together with these successes, the subsequent valiant service of the Pegasus represented an engineering triumph for its designers and manufacturer.

ABOVE The twin-row 18-cylinder 2,500hp Bristol Centaurus powers the RN Historic Flight's Sea Fury. As a brilliant successor to the Pegasus, the Centaurus was the last in a long line of Bristol radial engines. This family of engines evolved from the development of the Bristol Jupiter in the 1920s and '30s. Their quality and excellent performance, especially their reliability, were owed to the skill of their designer, Bristol's Sir Roy Fedden.

BRISTOL PEGASUS – TECHNICAL SPECIFICATION

Type	Supercharged, nine cylinders radially displaced, air-cooled and fitted with a tractor airscrew having a reduction gear ratio of 0.5:1.
Bore of cylinders	5¾in (146mm).
Stroke of piston	7½in (190.5mm).
Piston displacement (ie, swept volume)	1,755cu in (28.7 litres).
Compression ratio	5.5:1.
Horsepower (max)	775hp @ 2,525rpm and +2.0lb boost @ 4,500ft.
Supercharging	Medium, boost rated + 0.5lb/sq in, max + 2.0lb/sq in (at the above revs and altitude), impellor gear ratio 7:1.
Propulsion	geared, epicyclic with 0.5.1 reduction, left-hand tractor drive.
Fuel (as available)	originally 87 octane (DTD 230), now 100 octane Avgas.
Crankshaft and airscrew	tractor with left-hand (anti-clockwise) rotation looking from the rear.
Nett dry weight of engine	980lb.
Length of engine	4ft 6in approx (1.83m).
Overall diameter of engine	4ft 3in approx (1.52m).
Spark plugs	RS-14-3RS or R5-14-3R. Gap 0.012 to 0.015in. Advance 35 degrees BTC.
Magneto speed	9/8th of engine speed. Direction of rotation: anti-clockwise.
Valves and timing	intake and exhaust valves; timing.
Inlet valve:	Opening 12 degrees BTC.
	Closing 50 degrees ABC.
	Exhaust valve: Opening 65 degrees BBC.
	Closing 31 degrees ATC.

RIGHT Fairey three-blade fixed pitch propeller. This metal propeller is based on the American Reed design. It is non-featuring with the pitch formed through the twist built into the three blades.
(Copyright unknown)

Classification of Pegasus types

Bristol Aero Engines developed a numbering system by which key differences and characteristics could be identified. For instance, take the case of the Pegasus IIIM3 of 1935 that was fitted in the Swordfish Mark I – the 'III' gives us the engine series, the letter 'M' indicates a 'moderately' supercharged engine, and the final '3' denotes an airscrew reduction gear of 0.5 to 1.

This mark (initially rated at 690hp) was subsequently succeeded by the Pegasus 30, which gave 775hp and differed principally from its predecessor in having a sleeve crank pin-type big end.

Propeller

This is a Fairey-manufactured three-blade fixed pitch airscrew. Each of the blades is formed from a forged aluminium blank twisted to the requisite angle after heat treatment and shaping. Being of the fixed pitch type means the unit dispenses with the extra weight and complexity of constant speed or adjustable pitch mechanisms. The design is based on a US Reed design. The blades are aerodynamically profiled to an aerofoil section from their root ends to the propeller tips. The blades are then twisted to give an optimum pitch for all flight regimes from take-off to landing.

The propeller blades are held between two steel flanged clamping rings which fit over stepped root ends with the assembly fastened by bolts passed through holes in the blade roots. The blade/ring combination is bolted over a splined hub, which engages with the main engine shaft and the complete propeller assembly is covered with a metal spinner.

It must be stressed that each complete airscrew is an entity or individual unit, which is subject to fine balancing in both static and dynamic respects. Thus none of the major parts will be interchangeable with any other airscrew of the same type.

Cowling

The cowling is made of Duralumin and is in three parts to provide access to the engine for maintenance purposes. It is one of the earliest forms of cowling and is known as

a Townend Ring. This evolved from research undertaken by the eponymous scientist, which was carried out in the 1930s at the National Physical Laboratory, Teddington, near London. Dr H.C. Townend's work proceeded around the time that similar work was being done by NACA in the US. This research established the fact that not only was drag reduced by such a cowling, but cooling was also improved. In addition by giving attention to the cowling's shape, a measurable degree of forward lift could be obtained.

Eventually the later marks of the Pegasus engine on such types as the Vickers Wellington and the Short Sunderland would have enclosed cowlings, necessitating the provision of cooling gills. In addition, these engines incorporated baffles to further encourage airflow around the cylinders to give a greater cooling effect.

Exhaust

The leading edge of the Townend Ring faired into the engine cowling consists of an exhaust collector ring. This collects the products of combustion from all 18 exhaust ports, which gases are then discharged through a short exhaust pipe, fixed to the fuselage on its lower starboard side.

Later versions of the Swordfish were fitted with pierced exhaust pipes as a flame damping aid for night operations.

Engine mounts

The Pegasus is bolted to a flanged engine supporting ring, using 18 No. ⅜in steel bolts. The ring, which can be independently detached, is supported by 4 pyramidal

RIGHT Finned aluminium head. Note the depth of finning, carried across between the valve springs.

RIGHT Each cylinder has two inlet and two exhaust ports. The exhaust manifolds are joined to the collector ring, which forms the leading edge of the Townend Ring engine cowling.

RIGHT The crankshaft assembly is a solid steel forging. The two components on the left are joined by means of a maneton bolt tightened by using a special rig and tool. Requisite tightness of this was traditionally checked with a screw micrometer.

RIGHT Con rods. These are shown projecting through the crankcase housing with small ends ready to be connected to their respective pistons by gudgeon pins.

projections of the tubular fuselage framing attached at 12 points, at top bottom and middle locations on the front fireproof bulkhead (see Chapter 3).

Engine

Cylinders

These are constructed of steel with aluminium heads and with close-set fins to top and sides. Deep finning is a characteristic feature of the Pegasus engine. At around 1¾in (approx 4.6cm) the fins are up to twice the depth of those on the cylinders of some equivalent US radial engines.

Crankshaft

The crankshaft is constructed of a solid steel forging running in roller bearings. The crankcase provides support for the crankshaft and is of forged alloy with the cylinders bolted to its periphery. The master connecting rod links to No 6 cylinder.

Reduction gearing

This is of the Farman (or bevel planetary) type and comprises two crown wheels and three bevel pinions. This gearing is housed in a casting enclosing the crankshaft and bolted to the front of the engine directly behind the propeller.

BELOW Reduction gearing inside its housing. This is a planetary system comprising of two crown wheels connecting three bevel pinions.

FAR LEFT Reduction
gear with splined
propeller shaft. The
effect of the gearing is
to reduce the propeller
rpm by a ratio of 0.5:1
in the case of the IIIM3
series Pegasus engine.

LEFT As shown, each
piston is grooved
for five piston rings.
These provide gas-
tight sealing to aid
compression together
with control and
clearance of cylinder
oil.

Pistons

These are made of aluminium alloy. Five
rings are fitted in corresponding grooves
in the piston sides. They are manufactured
from iron. From the top downwards these
are (successively) two compression rings to
provide a gas-tight seal, an intermediate ring
with an oil control ring, and finally a scraper
ring to clear oil from the cylinder.

The piston rings play an important part in the
proper functioning of the engine. To that end each
is designed to provide a gas-tight fit in its location
down the side of the piston, while moving freely
and flexibly in its respective groove.

By their nature the piston rings will be subject
to wear and will therefore need to be replaced
at an appropriate stage in the maintenance and
overhaul cycle.

Valves and rocker arms

Each cylinder head incorporates two inlet and
two exhaust valve openings. The alloy exhaust
valves contain sodium in the stem as a heat
dispersing agent. Valve seats are screwed into
the exhaust and inlet ports.

A self-compensating device consisting of
a tie rod, located between the pushrods and
connected to the front ends of the rocker
boxes, maintains correct valve clearances by
offsetting heat expansion.

The 36 valves are opened by 18 pushrods.
Each is actuated by a cam sleeve on the
crankshaft. These are located between the
reduction gear and the crank rod and are
connected at their upper end to rockers,
which depress the valves. Return is effected
by sets of valve springs. Each set comprises
three different springs so as to accommodate
differing temperature.

Supercharger

This is located at the rear of the engine
assembly. A shaft, coaxial with the crankshaft,
drives a vaned impellor sending air under
pressure via a vaned diffuser into the cylinders,
at each induction stroke. A 10in-diameter
impellor is driven through intermediate gears
incorporating centrifugal clutches. This provision
allows the pilot to close the throttle without
overloading the supercharger gearing.

FAR LEFT Inlet
and exhaust valve
openings.

LEFT Valve springs.
The combination of
three concentric valve
sets per port ensures
precisely timed
opening and closing
for inlet and exhaust
purposes.

RIGHT Supercharger internal casting, showing the vanes on the back of the casing.

RIGHT Oil cooler. This overhead view shows how hot oil is led through the cooler (in effect a system of steel channels) and out into the slipstream to be cooled by the airflow along the fuselage.

RIGHT The blanking off of the lower forward section of the oil cooler is clearly seen in this photograph.

A boost control mechanism controls the response of the supercharger to take-off, climb and levelling out at optimum cruising height. Supercharger components (ie gearing, volutes and the impellor) are housed within a cast alloy casing bolted to the rear of the engine. At the normal speed of the engine the impellor will revolve at 14,000rpm.

Magnetos

These are manufactured by British Thomson Houston and are the SC9-5B model. Two are fitted at the rear of the engine and these are turned in an anti-clockwise direction at ⅝th engine speed.

Carburettor

This is of the Claudel Hobson AVT 80.B Duplex type, which supplies 42gal of fuel per hour at rated power. Depending on engine requirements the range of mixture control varies from 50% to 60%.

Lubrication

An oil pump delivers lubricant under a pressure of 60lb/sq in to the master rod, big end and articulated rod pin bearings, together with the cam gear, rear cover and reduction gear. All other lubrication within the engine is through splash effect.

The oil cooler is mounted externally on the starboard side of the fuselage behind the engine cowling. This comprises banks of tungum elements sweated to cross tubes which are curved outwards to catch the airflow. Part of the cooler is normally blanked off due to too great a cooling effect.

Starter

Several different methods were used for starting piston engines during the period in which the Swordfish was developed and in service. During the post-First World War era, the rotating spindle of the Hucks Starter, fitted in Model T Fords, taken off the main drive, could be seen being used for service aircraft.

Bristol engines including the Pegasus were fitted with a gas starter. Here, gas under pressure is fed into the cylinder, above the piston, thus serving to throw the engine. Later the modern monoplane fighters of the mid- to late 1930s availed themselves of battery starting, with power supplied by small mobile trolley accumulators. Alternatively, cartridge starters have been employed and these proved equally useful with first generation gas turbine engines.

An earlier form of starting mechanism was built into Bristol Pegasus engines. The engine of the Swordfish is provided with an inertia starter. This is hand operated, rotating a spindle by means of a detachable handle, normally stowed in the rear cockpit. The handle locates in a socket high up on the port side of the engine and connects via a chain drive with a rotating flywheel. At 13,000rpm the device enables inertia energy to be released which will turn the engine over to initiate a start.

One set of ancillaries not present in aircraft of this generation was that providing hydraulic power. The place of such a system as a source of power is taken by a pneumatic system fed by a compressor driven through connection with the crankshaft. This feeds compressed air to an air bottle located within the fuselage.

System

Fuel and oil

The fuel and oil tanks are of sheet metal construction using 18swg aluminium, welded at the seams and located between the fire bulkhead and the cockpit. Fuel is supplied to the carburettor either by means of gravity or by activation of a fuel pump. Oil is fed to the engine under pump pressure, with return via external oil cooler. This is aided by a scavenge pump. (See the specification above for capacities etc.)

When operational the Swordfish could be

ABOVE Inertia starter chain drive. Using a detachable rotating handle, the sprocket in the centre of the photograph is turned by chain, accelerating a flywheel that provides inertia for starting.

FAR LEFT The hand-starting procedure in operation. The degree of initial inertia in the mechanism, coupled with the rather precarious position required of the ground-crew, presumes that at least two if not three team members participate in the start-up. *(FAA Museum)*

LEFT Compressed air storage bottle. This serves as a reservoir for the pneumatic braking system. Air is compressed through an ancillary drive off the engine's crankshaft.

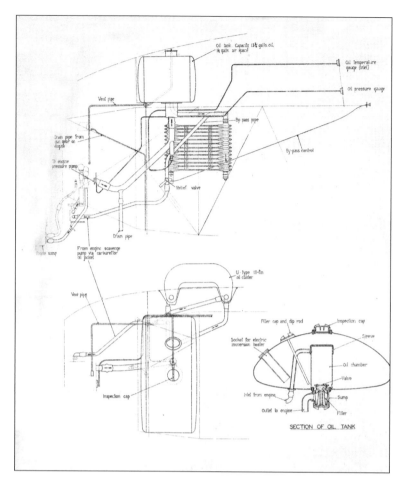

ABOVE Main fuel tank (left, behind oil cooler), oil tank (top right) and oil cooler (centre). Fuel is fed to the engine from the main tank (155gal) via a smaller (12½gal) gravity-operated feeder tank. With a two-tank system, diligent monitoring of fuel levels is necessary so as to identify when changeover should be effected.

ABOVE Oil system. The external oil cooler or radiator is a prominent feature on the starboard side of the Swordfish's engine cowling. Being too effective in all but tropical operating conditions, it is usually blanked off in its lower part. (AP1517/RNHF)

RIGHT Overload fuel system, mid-cockpit type. The overload or auxiliary fuel tank was fitted in the observer's position and was made from aluminium sheet. Capacity was 60gal. (AP1517/RNHF)

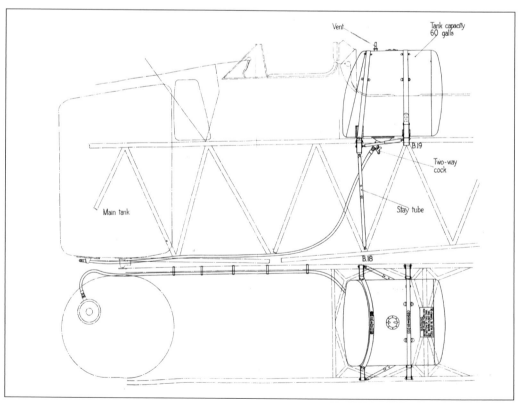

fitted with so-called 'overload' fuel provision. Long-range sorties and/or extra weight of stores might dictate the need for extra fuel. This need could be met in two ways. The more common arrangement was to provide an extra (auxiliary) 60gal tank located on bearers in the mid-cockpit (in the observer's position). Alternatively, if the aircraft was being used in a non-torpedo role, a 69gal tank could be carried in the torpedo crutches under the fuselage.

Fuel pump

This is of the Bristol Vane type and is driven directly off the engine at engine speed.

Fuel is fed by this pump from a main tank positioned directly behind the engine firewall. This simple configuration dispenses with the long fuel runs associated with wing fuel storage. In addition a much smaller gravity feed header tank is located immediately ahead of the pilot's position. This can be selected by the pilot in case of fuel pump failure. The fuel gauge can be visually sighted from the cockpit.

Electrics and ignition

Current from magnetos is supplied to the twin sparking plugs of each cylinder via high tension (HT) leads. There are two magnetos and these are located on each side and at the rear of the engine. Double provision is mandatory. These magnetos are driven off the engine and feed current to the ignition system via a contact breaker, condenser and distributor, which are mounted behind the engine. The contact breaker and distributor are also driven directly off the engine. The ignition sequence by cylinder number is 1, 3, 5, 7, 9, 2, 4, 6 and 8 timed at 35 degrees BTC.

Much attention has been paid to the problems of the insulation of the HT leads running to the spark plugs. The leads are hermetically sealed and sheathed in earthed conducive steel braiding. This form of protection suppresses any radio interference.

A 500-watt engine-driven 12-volt generator provides current for lighting, including the requirements of the landing lamps in the leading edges of the bottom mainplanes as well as for landing flares and gun heating. Current is also supplied to the wireless installation motor generator and the camera motor.

ABOVE Main fuel tank. This view shows the underside of the main fuel tank when in situ. Note the braided fuel pipeline and the additional torsional cross-bracing to the fuselage framing, needed on account of the extra weight.

BELOW Engine removal reveals fuel and oil supply lines, electric leads and pneumatic linkages grouped in a seeming haphazard manner behind the fire bulkhead.

Chapter Five

Restoring a Swordfish

With such priceless aviation heritage at stake it is not surprising that so much dedicated effort and expertise has been expended by corporations and individuals to keeping the Royal Navy Historic Flight's aircraft flying. Highly specialised engineering and maintenance skills are needed to keep the Swordfish airworthy, but thankfully these are qualities that can be found in abundance on the Flight at RNAS Yeovilton.

OPPOSITE W5856, the world's oldest surviving Swordfish, sits awaiting paintwork in the paint shop at RNAS Yeovilton, **11 October 2013.** *(Mick Jennings)*

Spitfire, Hurricane and Mustang restorers and their erstwhile owners are in a sense lucky. They are able to draw on a substantial body of knowledge, accumulated as an outcome of the many successful restorations of their chosen type that have taken place.

Conversely, with just a handful of Swordfish surviving worldwide in museums and only two that are airworthy (at the time of writing), there is scant experience of the work and techniques necessary to revive a 'Stringbag'. Fortunately there is a very good record of the restoration work undertaken in 1990 by BAE Systems to veteran Mark I, W5856, so that the knowledge has been passed on to the Royal Navy Historic Flight in connection with their work.

W5856 is a Blackburn-built Mark I, the oldest extant version of its type, and a survivor from a small number of ex-Royal Canadian Air Force Swordfish. Originally delivered to the Royal Navy it was transferred to the RAF and served at RAF Manston before it was shipped to Canada. Struck off charge by the RCAF in 1946, this particular aircraft was eventually sold in Ontario to an Alabama farmer. After an unsuccessful attempt to convert it for crop dusting W5856 was acquired in 1977 by Sir William Roberts for his historic aircraft collection at the Strathallan Castle estate near Auchterarder in Scotland.

Unfortunately W5856 came with several problems: the main spar and fuselage framing in particular had areas of severe corrosion. However, after purchase the aircraft was stripped down and its condition assessed before receiving preparatory care from resident enthusiasts. The aircraft was eventually purchased from the collection by British Aerospace (BAe) in 1990 with the aim of presenting it to the Fly Navy Trust.

On acquiring the Swordfish BAe faced its first challenge – the need to transfer its precious new acquisition to a place of restoration. Unfazed, the company took delivery of a carefully dismantled W5856 on 13 December 1990 and transported three truckloads of vintage aeroplane 400 miles to its factory at Brough on the north bank of the River Humber.

BAe Brough's normal expertise was as far removed from Swordfish design and construction as it could be. Its workforce was used to dealing with jet airframes like the Buccaneer and the Hawk and was thus two or more generations removed from familiarity with the 'Stringbag's' method of manufacture. Thus, it was clear from the outset that successful restoration would rely on a mixture of adapting in-house skills to simpler, more manual techniques, and the buying in of more specialised expertise from elsewhere.

Initial surveys of the airframe revealed a reassuring degree of sound metal. However, from this point onwards critical decisions had to be made about what had been inherited from Strathallan. Each individual component would be classified as a) for retention, usually after testing; or b) for replacement. Replacement was often easier said than done. If usable spares could not be found, then the expensive task of one-off manufacture might have to be contemplated.

Preparation stages

A start was made on one of the more laborious initial tasks, that of cleaning all parts to be retained. As was realised, flaking paintwork can only be effectively removed by hand. No machine was available that could undertake this work as successfully as the human operative.

Components of W5856 exhibited a wide range of damage, depending on the nature of their constituent materials. Any non-ferrous metals were most likely to retain their integrity while textile survivals were often the

BELOW NF389 arrives at BAE Systems at Brough in January 1999 for its rebuild. On 6 June 1994 the aircraft took part in the 50th anniversary commemoration of the D-Day landings. To mark the involvement of Swordfish in Operation 'Overlord' she wears the white paint scheme with distinctive D-Day invasion stripes. *(BAE Systems)*

worst affected. The oft-quoted miraculous relighting of Brooklands Museum's Wellington tail light is a testament to the possibility that even submersion in a Scottish loch may not necessarily mean a part cannot survive. In fact the reaction of those faced with the task of cleaning and inspection of Swordfish parts was that it was like working on wreckage dredged up from the *Titanic*!

Testing of parts

The next stage involved the testing of parts to be retained. Here the up-to-date – and in some cases the cutting edge of BAe's technological resources – came into play. Three critical non-destructive techniques available at Brough were used at this point:

- A technique that represented an adaptation of the medical X-ray process. In this instance corrosion or cracking shows up on the exposed plastic film when laid on a light box.
- The so-called 'Magic Eye'. A camera probe can be used to explore the interior of metal tubing or other non-visible parts of a component.
- Magnetic Particle Testing. With this technique, black-inked magnetised particles are seen to jump around on white-painted metal components. Their movements can indicate cracks and fissures, including inclusions which may date from the original manufacturing process.

Research and spares procurement

With the Royal Navy Historic Flight's airworthy Swordfish (LS326) used as a template for the restoration process, the Brough team made several visits to the Flight hangar at RNAS Yeovilton so that photographs could effectively fill in the gaps caused by missing drawings. An important aspect of these visits was that of ensuring complete uniformity of controls and instrumentation between the two aircraft. This was important to the Flight's aircrew who required complete commonality when flying either aircraft.

When BAe staff visited Yeovilton they took

the opportunity to check with the Royal Navy Historic Flight to see whether any deficiencies in components back at Brough could be made good from the Flight's stock of spares. As an example the Flight was able to supply a Pegasus exhaust collector ring, otherwise unavailable to the BAe team.

Wing repair

Tests revealed damage to the upper boom-type flange of a mainplane spar. The technique in this case was that recommended in AP1517 (the official repairs instructions). This involved making a splint of the same material and profile as the damaged boom section and then close-riveting this across the defect, with substantial overlap each side of the repair. With the mainplanes being subject to flying stresses the decision was taken to provide further riblets behind the wing leading edge. These were inserted between those already existing in order to help preserve the necessary aerofoil.

When the tail and elevator were inspected it was clear they would not submit readily to selective repair, so the decision was taken to completely rebuild them. Repairs having been completed the wing elements had to be weighed. This was easily carried out utilising an overhead gantry available within the works.

All repair and replacement work was subject to the scrutiny and approval of the Ministry of Defence Quality Assurance Officer.

BELOW This photograph was taken during the early 1990s restoration of W5856 at Brough. The familiar yellow 'radioactive' warning sign suggests non-destructive testing was taking place.
(Copyright unknown)

ABOVE W5856 in her distinctive circa 1939 markings applied to her following restoration at Brough in the late 1990s. They represent an 810 NAS commander's Swordfish as embarked on HMS *Ark Royal*. *(RNHF)*

ABOVE By 1940 front-line Swordfish had been treated to a temperate camouflage scheme on their upper surfaces. *(Copyright unknown)*

ABOVE LS326 wearing D-Day invasion stripes for the 40th anniversary of D-Day in 1984. Her overall paint scheme at that time was a hybrid of different styles and not strictly accurate. *(Jonathan Falconer collection)*

ABOVE RIGHT Black-painted Swordfish Mark IIIs (NF374 'NH-M', NF343 'NH-Q' and 'NH-L') of 119 Squadron RAF, B58/Knokke le Zoute, Belgium, flying in loose formation over the North Sea. In early 1945 119 Squadron's Swordfish carried out night searches for the German Seehund and Biber midget submarines. *(IWM CL2290)*

RIGHT The new paint scheme proposal for W5856 for the 2014 air show season. *(RNHF)*

The first period of FAA service saw the Swordfish furnished with a quite wide range of insignia and marking. Apart from the individual aircraft's unique serial number and the standard roundels of the period, markings could indicate the parent carrier, the squadron and individual aircraft letter and whether it was the personal aircraft of a flight or squadron commander. Carrier identity would be displayed through broad-coloured diagonal stripes down fuselage sides (for example, yellow for HMS *Glorious*, blue/red/blue for *Ark Royal*) often with a call sign number overlaid on the band.

Camouflage was introduced on the outbreak of war. Aircraft identification became a more discreet affair. There followed some degree of trial and error to identify the best colour treatment to suppress outline or silhouette. Initially FAA machines fell in with RAF practice so that temperate green and grey on the upper wing, tailplane and fuselage surfaces would be combined with sea grey on the lower fuselage and under the wings.

However, when operating over the sea this combination proved unsatisfactory and from late 1941 both FAA and RAF Coastal Command aircraft were painted in slate grey and extra dark grey on the upper surfaces and sides and white on the lower fuselage and under-wing areas.

Two further changes took place with the Swordfish. Black and white D-Day stripes were applied to wings and fuselage in June 1944. Finally, during its swansong contribution in 1945 conducting night patrols over the North Sea, the Mark III ASV Mark X-equipped aircraft of the two RAF squadrons tasked with this valuable work were painted overall in matt black, ensuring that the Swordfish went out on a slightly sinister note.

ABOVE **Tug Wilson, one of RNHF's stalwart maintainers, presents a full set of Pegasus cylinder heads, complete with their valve assemblies in situ.** *(Jonathan Falconer)*

The engine

While initial work was proceeding on the airframe, consideration was being given to the restoration of the engine, the redoubtable Bristol Pegasus IIIM3. Engine expert Peter Dean of Rolls-Royce, who was tasked with the job of restoring the Pegasus to full working order, sought help from Royal Navy Historic Flight's stock of spares.

Serviceable components such as crankshafts and crankcases and supercharger elements were taken back to Filton, Bristol.

Brough spread its information net quite widely. As an example Swordfish NF389, originally based at Lee-on-the-Solent (HMS *Daedalus*), was also inspected as another useful 'template'.

Instruments and rigging

Instrumentation is an aspect of aviation engineering where dramatic changes have taken place since the introduction of the Swordfish into service in the 1930s. To maintain authenticity the Second World War analogue cockpit instruments were restored.

Rigging is another example of strict adherence to authentic repair. Provision of rigging wires involved BAe out-sourcing specialist manufacturing skills. Bruntons of Musselburgh provided the answer. They made a range of replacement wires and cables for W5856, using 50-year-old machinery, involving just a slight departure from 1930s/1940s practice, in this case substituting splicing for the

ABOVE Cockpit instrumentation is refitted in W5856 during the later stages of her restoration at Brough. Noteworthy in this photograph is the pyramidal strutting which supports the cabane – or upper mainplane centre section – the pilot's compass and the sockets for the Patent Fairey Fasteners on the fuselage framing. *(BAE Systems)*

ABOVE Anchorage points for rigging wires adjoining the base of an interplane strut. Note the drawn streamlined profile of the two wires. *(Jonathan Falconer)*

crimping method used of old. To give an idea of the strength of cable manufacture, they were made to have a breaking point of 7.4 tons.

Fabric covering

A large proportion of the Swordfish airframe is fabric covered. It is a specialised task and one which again had to be outsourced in the case of W5856. David and Pat Fenton of

RIGHT Fabric covering of the upper fuselage as seen from the inside. An early coat of dope is visible through the Irish linen fabric. *(Jonathan Falconer)*

Hornet Aviation at Seaton Ross, Yorkshire, have been repairing light aircraft since the early 1970s and have completed a number of restorations of 1930s and '40s aircraft as well as restoring components for the Royal Navy Historic Flight's Swordfish. Key factors in fabric covering are the quality of materials and accuracy in its cutting, with the minimum of waste and the need to avoid the fabric being exposed to fluctuations in temperature and humidity. Once the fabric has been obtained, the covering process should take place expeditiously to avoid any such changes affecting the integrity of the material.

Taking the example of the wing mainplanes, a 'bag' is made and shaped to the wing outline, and then it is sewn in such a way that one side is left open. The wing structure is then inserted and the fabric pulled taut so that its extremities are tight against the trailing edges and wingtips.

It is then sewn into its bag, once again with precautionary tautening. In the case of the mainplanes on W5856 the stitching, which always uses waxed thread, was worked along the perimeter using a curved needle, with $\frac{1}{8}$in gaps and a lock stitch every 2in.

The next process is to anchor the canvas to the wing structure. This is done by looping the waxed thread from the top wing surface through to the underside and back again so that the fabric is stitched and knotted to the appropriate rib.

THIS PAGE (1) This stage comprises a wraparound process with the fabric drawn taut across the wing framing. (2) The shape of wingtips is described in narrow-diameter tube, lending itself to the use of the Jubilee Clips as restraint. (3) Fabric is held lapped over wing roots by the simple expedient of masking tape. (4) The presence of slats along the upper mainplane leading edge must be taken into account in the wing re-covering process. (5) Fabric covering represents a complete envelope including wing roots. (6) Slinging mainplanes during the covering/doping processes prevents undue distortion of the structure.

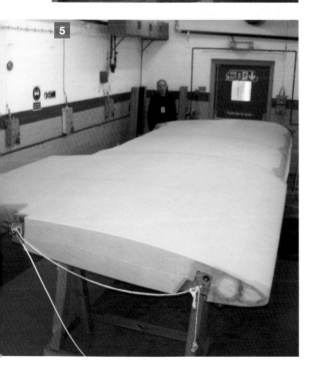

RIGHT Canvas is anchored to the wing structure by looping the waxed thread. This is the view inside the wing. While in production at Brough and Sherburn in Elmet during the Second World War, this threading task would have been performed by two women workers, one on each side of the wing. *(Jonathan Falconer)*

One other example of necessary out-sourcing is that of the leatherwork. Hugh Macrae of Farnborough Aircraft Interiors was called in to undertake the work on the Swordfish. Its worn-out crew seats and the leather trim along cockpit sills needed replacement. Although this was relatively straightforward and in keeping with original practice, modern regulations required special non-combustible material for the seat fillings.

Doping the fabric-covered elements is a somewhat lengthy process. After the first coat of red oxide medium-tautness nitro-cellulose dope has dried the exposed nap is removed by gentle abrasion before two further coats are applied. This red dope provides the first degree

RIGHT Note the built-in handholds along the wingtip of the mainplane. *(Hornet Aviation)*

FAR RIGHT Completed and painted upper starboard wing ready for attachment. *(Jonathan Falconer)*

RIGHT, FAR RIGHT AND BELOW LEFT Insignia painting on W5856, November 2013. The complete masking of non-paintable areas is a necessary precaution prior to the spraying of coats of dope, carried out in the paint shop at RNAS Yeovilton. *(Mick Jennings)*

FAR RIGHT W5856 emerges with dark grey upper surfaces. *(Howard Read)*

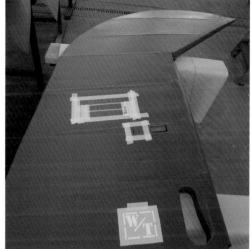

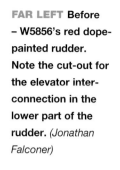

FAR LEFT Before – W5856's red dope-painted rudder. Note the cut-out for the elevator inter-connection in the lower part of the rudder. (Jonathan Falconer)

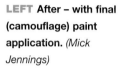

LEFT After – with final (camouflage) paint application. (Mick Jennings)

FAR LEFT Painted top wing centre section. The circular recess in wing leading edge (in the foreground) is for the identification light mounting. (Jonathan Falconer)

LEFT Wing sections under wraps inside the RNHF hangar to prevent damage to the paintwork. (Jonathan Falconer)

LEFT W5856 is wheeled out of the paint shop at RNAS Yeovilton on 7 February 2014. (Mick Jennings)

of tautness and protects the organic (flax) fabric (Irish Linen) from biological attack. A further two coats of aluminium medium- to high-tautness dope is applied providing the final tautness and protecting the fabric from ultra-violet attack. Only now can the final colour cellulose paint finish be applied and in the case of W5856 this comprises ten different colours and a final coat of gloss clear dope to provide a durable long-lasting finish that can be easily maintained.

Final assembly

Wing fitting can be a lengthy process and correct alignment is critical. The required dihedral of each mainplane and its incidence must be achieved by adjusting the rigging wires. The correct geometry for wing folding adds a further layer of complexity to an already difficult task. To this end the mainplane, stub and cabane wing roots must meet perfectly when the wings are spread.

The propeller

Propeller repair is another area best dealt with by specialists. In this case H + S Aviation at Portsmouth were called in to undertake the work. Balance is a critical factor with propellers, while correct alignment and equal blade weight are also important considerations.

Correction of imbalance between the three fixed blades of the Swordfish is not always a straightforward business. In the case of W5856 the propeller had already been painted when it was found that it was slightly out of balance. The options available were to strip all paint from each blade and hope the extra weight of an additional coat would literally tip the balance, or as an alternative to selectively regrind a blade or blades. In the event the latter course of action was chosen and proved to be successful.

Finale

With plenty of space and fairly open surroundings, ground running and engine tests could be carried out close to where the aircraft had been restored. Engine checks and the testing of controls were an instant success. On 12 May 1993 some two and a half years' work was crowned with success when W5856 rolled gently forward along the grass runway, dipped a little and then soared away in a gently banked turn cheered on by a small knot of dedicated work people who had given it wings and rebirth. Per Ardua.

RIGHT W5856 in her pre-war colour scheme. *(RNHF)*

Restoration 2009–14

The Swordfish design, like those of all historic aircraft, has its virtues but can also present one or two vices. One such vice relates to the main spar. Due perhaps to problems in sourcing materials, particularly under wartime conditions, this critical component was fabricated in a composite manner rather than being provided in a single homogenous form. The problem lies in what are called the flanges. The classic 'I' shape of the beam relies on flanges at top and bottom to stiffen and strengthen the structural member for it to support its loads without undue deflection. The designers of the Swordfish main spar saw fit to create their flanges out of rolled metal sheet – in effect, two paired tubes serve as the spar flanges top and bottom. Unfortunately they built in a persistent flaw. Due, possibly, to a shortage of the appropriate metals in a suitable gauge to form the rolled tubes (or maybe for weight reasons) they were built up of two thicknesses. The very thin gap thus created, of almost capillary dimensions, forms the perfect moisture trap. Swordfish main spars have been plagued by this design defect since the early days of their existence.

Subject as it was to one of the most thorough restoration projects of recent times, it might have been expected that W5856 would provide many years of uninterrupted flying service for the RN Historic Flight, but this was not to be. Ten years after she was presented to the RNHF by BAE Systems after her restoration at Brough (see above) the problem of main spar corrosion reared its head again. With a generosity that says much for the fraternal nature of the British aircraft industry, BAE Systems offered to build a complete set of new wings.

The enforced retirement of W5856 was seen by the Royal Navy Historic Flight as an opportunity for root and branch overhaul of airframe and engine. The value of the skills developed by the maintainer team has come to the fore in this situation. Apart from the overhaul of the Pegasus engine, which was at its due date in times of flying hours, much of the work required has been undertaken in-house. Such tasks as painting and minor fuselage repairs have been entrusted to the maintainers. At time of publication the wings, duly presented by their benefactor, BAE Systems, await assembly and attachment to the fuselage. The engine with its propeller has been undergoing overhaul, with Delta Airmotive in Waterlooville, Hampshire. Even here, the specialist skills of others have had to be drawn upon. In this case cylinders and pistons have had to be subcontracted by them to firms elsewhere in the country.

With summer 2014 coming on, W5856 stands on the threshold of a new lease of life once again.

Chapter Six

The Royal Navy Historic Flight's Swordfish

The Royal Navy Historic Flight has three Fairey Swordfish aircraft in its collection – Swordfish Mark I, W5856, the oldest surviving Swordfish in the world, Swordfish Mark II, LS326, which served with 836 NAS embarked in MAC ships during the long and bitterly fought Battle of the Atlantic, and Swordfish Mark III, NF389, which is currently preserved awaiting an opportunity to be rebuilt.

OPPOSITE W5856 and LS326 together in close formation. At this time W5856 had recently been restored and was flying in the peacetime colours of the CO of 810 NAS as embarked on HMS *Ark Royal*. *(RNHF)*

The Royal Navy Historic Flight is uniquely privileged to own three of these historic machines, representing all three marks of Swordfish. Given favourable circumstances it has been possible in recent years to present two of the three aircraft in the air at certain air displays and Royal Navy commemorative events. One such occasion, which the author was privileged to witness, served to underline the priceless value of these machines to naval aviation heritage. This was the 1994 D-Day celebration held in the Solent. This important event saw LS326 and W5856 both take off from the now decommissioned Royal Naval Air Station HMS *Daedalus*. One could watch them as they made fly-past runs alongside the giant nuclear-powered super carrier USS *George Washington* anchored off the Isle of Wight. What a salutary experience for the young US Navy personnel on board, unfamiliar possibly with the names *Bismarck*, Taranto, *Scharnhorst* and *Gneisenau*.

Turning to the origins of the Royal Navy Historic Flight's Swordfish, while the Fairey Aviation Company was responsible for design and initial manufacture of Swordfish, the Flight's three machines are in fact all 'Blackfish' (aircraft that were constructed by Blackburn's). These were rolled out in the early 1940s from their factory at Sherburn in Elmet in Yorkshire after production had been switched from Fairey's factory in the south of England.

W5856

This is a Mark I and was one of 415 aircraft known to have been built at the Yorkshire factory during 1941. Thus, W5856 was one of the first of the batches produced after Blackburn's had taken over production responsibility from Fairey's the previous year. This makes her the oldest known Swordfish of the dozen or so still intact around the world.

Initially the aircraft was based in the Mediterranean, possibly undertaking patrols in the Straits of Gibraltar, which were an important task of Rock-based aircraft towards the end of 1942 and into early 1943. Details of her service in the Mediterranean theatre during this period are unclear although it is known she eventually accrued around 500 flying hours.

However, we do know that W5856 was one of several Swordfish that were eventually transferred to the Royal Canadian Navy in 1944 and shipped across the Atlantic. Once in Canada Swordfish aircraft played an important part in the Commonwealth Air Training Plan. They were used to train FAA telegraphist air gunners (TAGs) at the RCN Air Station, Yarmouth, Nova Scotia. Eventually their second-line duties included towing target drogues.

Ex-RCAF/RCN aircraft were sold off after the Second World War and when purchased by private owners they were often in a dilapidated state. A small number were brought back

RIGHT Aerial view of W5856. W5856 is the oldest surviving Swordfish in the world being a Mark I version built in 1941 by Blackburn's at their Yorkshire works. *(RNHF)*

across the Atlantic. One of these was Swordfish W5856, which was acquired by the Strathallan Collection in 1977.

British Aerospace (BAe) bought it from the collection's owner Sir William Roberts and the early 1990s saw it restored by them to flying condition. Details of the process of restoration and the various techniques and procedures adopted in a two-year-long programme of restoration carried out at the BAe factory at Brough are given in Chapter 5.

W5856 was test-flown after successful completion of the work in May 1993 and was gifted to the Royal Navy Historic Flight in 1996. Unfortunately, as might be expected after its post-war maltreatment, the aircraft eventually succumbed to further corrosion problems. Wing spar corrosion caused her to be grounded in 2003. In a splendid generous gesture, BAE Systems (created out of the merger of Marconi Electronic Systems and British Aerospace in 1999) came to the rescue. A complete set of wings was built at Brough. At the time of writing (2014) the new wings are being assembled and reunited with the fuselage together with its Bristol Pegasus engine.

In commemoration of the attacks on the *Bismarck*, W5856 has been repainted to represent an aircraft of 820 NAS, which participated in the crippling of the German battleship in 1941.

LS326

Perhaps the best known of the Royal Navy Historic Flight trio because of its long record of aerial display with the Flight, LS326 is a Swordfish Mark II and left the Blackburn works at Sherburn in Elmet in 1943. The Swordfish Mark II was distinguished by its rocket projectile (R/P) capability. To this end LS326 was provided with strengthened wings and the undersides of her lower mainplanes were clad with metal to protect them from the fierce flame and heat emitted by the projectiles.

LS326 is a veteran of the North Atlantic convoys and the Merchant Aircraft Carriers (MAC ships). A single large NAS, 836 based at RNAS Maydown in Northern Ireland, furnished the small Swordfish complements of the MAC ships. It is known that she served in two of these vessels,

the grain ship *Empire MacCallum* and the tanker *Rapana*. The latter entered service in October 1943 and was the first converted tanker to do so. LS326 was one of a flight of four Swordfish normally embarked for convoy duty. Without doubt they would have been subject to the effects of extreme exposure during the Atlantic crossing since, with no hangar available on these tanker conversions, the flight would have had to remain on deck throughout the voyage.

Empire MacCullum entered service in December 1943 and was previously a grain carrier. As such (and unlike the tankers) she and her sister ships incorporated a hangar as part of their conversion, ensuring that LS326 and the other embarked Swordfish were spared the worst ravages of the weather and could be serviced and maintained under cover.

It is not known whether LS326 saw action,

ABOVE LS326 over the flooded Somerset countryside in 2013. This watery scene would be repeated in 2014, with even more calamitous effects. The earlier Second World War temperate grey-green camouflage on LS326 would have integrated the Swordfish that much more effectively with the landscape mosaic than its present mixture of greys and white under surfaces. *(Crown Copyright)*

LEFT MAC ship HMS *Rapana*. Originally built in Holland, this 16,000-ton 12kt oil tanker conversion was home to LS326 for a short period, along with three other 836 NAS Swordfish. All these aircraft were stored on deck during their North Atlantic convoy duty. *(FAA Museum)*

but at least one attack is recorded for each of the MAC ships. It is generally accepted that the presence of the Swordfish on anti-submarine patrols armed with their fearsome A/P rockets acted as a powerful deterrent to U-boat attacks on convoys.

LS326 was fortunate. She was bought by the Fairey Aviation Company in May 1947 and used by them for various company purposes, including on occasion being flown by the company's legendary ex-FAA Chief Test Pilot Peter Twiss. For a while she was enrolled on the civil register as G-AJVH and was rebuilt on the orders of Sir Richard Fairey during the 1950s.

An opportunity to be seen by a much larger audience came along at the end of the 1950s when LS326 along with Swordfish Mark III, NF389, was recruited for a starring role in the

ABOVE LS326 as G-AJVH. Thanks to the wisdom of Sir Richard Fairey this machine was saved from the scrapyard. Once acquired by his firm it earned its living as a company hack. LS326 achieved film fame when, with NF389, it turned in a star performance in *Sink the Bismarck!*

BELOW *Sink the Bismarck* starred Kenneth More and Dana Wynter and was one of a series of post-war British war films which highlighted the drama of the Royal Navy in action in the Second World War. Little fiction was added and the role of the Fleet Air Arm and the Swordfish NAS was given due credit. *(Copyright unknown)*

BELOW HMS *Centaur*, a 'Hermes'-class aircraft carrier launched in 1947, was the best ship the film-makers could find to fill the roles of HMS *Victorious* and HMS *Ark Royal* for the take-off and landing-on sequences in the film. NF389 is in the foreground with LS326 behind. *(FAA Museum)*

ABOVE LS326, flown by the famous FAA pilot and Fairey test pilot Lt Cdr Peter Twiss, landing on HMS *Centaur* during filming for *Sink the Bismarck!* in April 1959. Twiss became well known when he gained the World Speed Record in the Fairey Delta 2 along the south coast in 1956, achieving a speed of 1,132mph. A Royal Navy S.51 Dragonfly helicopter can be seen hovering astern. *(Cdr T.A. Handley/FAA Museum)*

ABOVE The two veteran Swordfish LS326 (5A) and NF389 (5B, alias LS423) are seen flying in formation during the filming of the *Bismarck* movie. *(FAA Museum)*

film *Sink the Bismarck!* She was re-liveried as '5A', thus representing one of the 836 NAS Swordfish that crippled the German battleship in May 1941.

However, as a result of the reorganisation and amalgamation that took place in the British aerospace industry during the early post-war

RIGHT AND BELOW LS326 lands on HMS *Hermes* in the early 1960s. Note the Ship's Flight Whirlwind HAS 7 helicopter (XK935) in the background. This is probably the last time a Swordfish operated off a carrier deck.
(Copyright unknown)

ABOVE NF389 on static display at an air show in August 1974. (VLR via Keith Wilson)

NF389

A Blackburn-built Mark III, this aircraft began its service career in April 1944. For much of its life while on charge it was based in south Hampshire, first at Gosport with the ATDU and subsequently when used for flying displays at HMS *Daedalus*, Lee-on-the-Solent.

NF389 took part in the 1994 D-Day celebrations but was taken to BAE Systems at Brough in 1999 for them to undertake a rebuild. The aircraft is currently with the Royal Navy Historic Flight at RNAS Yeovilton, currently not airworthy.

The Royal Navy Historic Flight and its displays

Like many other heritage initiatives the Flight had its origins in the actions of a small number of companies and private individuals. The first arrival was LS326, given to the Royal Navy by Westland in late 1960. Later, in 1971, similar generosity was displayed by Hawker Siddeley, which donated the almost restored Hawker Sea Fury FB11. RNAS Yeovilton's Heron Flight completed the work to airworthy standard and added it to the already popular Swordfish.

period Fairey and its assets, including the Swordfish, were absorbed by Westland Aircraft Ltd. Eventually, in September 1960 that company (itself with a tradition of building naval aircraft) presented LS326 to the Royal Navy Historic Flight.

LS326, like W5856, has suffered from the effects of corrosion. Wing spar construction is one of the most vulnerable aspects of Swordfish design. The discovery of this problem in the aircraft in 1999 prompted another generous gesture by BAE Systems, with that company providing new sparred wings enabling the aircraft to take to the air again in 2010.

A further historic FAA aircraft was soon to join the inventory. While on a visit to Australia in 1967 some of the crew of HMS *Victorious* had spotted a Fairey Firefly AS5, which was promptly bought for £160! The Firefly was restored at RNAS Yeovilton and, with its three historic aircraft able to fly again, the Royal Navy Historic Flight came into being.

A succession of gifts and loans followed. Such is the esteem in which the FAA and its Historic Flight is held that there appears to be no bounds to the generosity of companies and individuals towards them. Even governments have given their support, an example being the gift of a Hawker Sea Fury T20 trainer in 1976 by the Federal Republic of Germany.

The greatest support has been provided by BAE Systems and its predecessors. Two additional Swordfish have been given by the company and BAE Systems at Brough has been instrumental over the years in carrying out restoration and rebuild work to the Swordfish when this has been required.

BELOW LS326 and Hawker Sea Fury VX281 outside the RNHF hangar in 2013. Apart from its spectacular performance as a display aircraft, maintaining a Sea Fury in flying condition serves to commemorate the role played by the Royal Navy and the Fleet Air Arm with this aircraft during the Korean War of the early 1950s. (Jonathan Falconer)

In the early days both aircrew and ground crew were drawn from serving Royal Navy personnel. In recent years maintenance has become a civilian function while utilising the acquired servicing skills and experience of former servicemen.

Aircrew remain drawn from serving FAA personnel. All are volunteers. When displaying the aircraft they are on duty but this is done in their own time. Much effort is devoted to training and practice – it must be remembered that their normal 'mounts' are modern jet aircraft or helicopters.

Enthusiasm for historic aircraft is a prerequisite for selection to join the Flight. It also requires skills and commitment of a unique kind to master the special requirements posed by piston-engine propeller-driven aircraft. Even more so to adjust to the problems posed in the handling of a tail-dragger aircraft with its poor visibility on the ground and its particular take-off and landing characteristics.

Members of the flying team are required to maintain a minimum number of flying hours on these aircraft. This figure is set by Navy Command but to this end the Flight has its own trainer on which pilots can log part of the Service requirement. This is a de Havilland Chipmunk T10 (WK608), a fully aerobatic aircraft that was once the standard *ab initio* trainer of the RAF and the FAA.

Training on the Chipmunk has been complemented by experience on other historic aircraft kindly loaned for training purposes by private individual owners. In this way Royal Navy Historic Flight pilots have been able to further hone their skills on aircraft such as the Percival Provost, the North American Harvard and the Jet Provost.

Royal Navy Historic Flight pilots build up their hours on tail-draggers and then have a continuity flight on the Swordfish. They must have five hours on type before they can display in public. Authorisation is given to display at public events after a performance in front of the Royal Navy Aircraft Operating Authority (AOA).

There are strict rules relating to flying currency. Two pilots will be tasked to perform in the Swordfish. If there is a gap of more than eight days between displays, pilots have to practise their display again before they next

ABOVE The de Havilland Canada Chipmunk T.10 had a long and distinguished career as the principal *ab initio* trainer of the RAF and Fleet Air Arm. It performs a valuable service for the RNHF today by providing flight experience and continuation training for pilots who are likely to be more familiar with modern machines. The pilots of the Flight tasked with displaying the Swordfish or Sea Fury are required to maintain a minimum number of hours on 'tail-dragger' propeller-driven aircraft. The Flight's Chipmunk WK608 is pictured here with LS326 in March 2012. *(Lee Howard)*

LEFT Mick Jennings of the Flight points to repairs on the port wing fabric of the Chipmunk. Mick is a member of an all-civilian team of maintainers who utilise their considerable skills, based on service experience, to maintain and overhaul the RNHF fleet to the highest standards. *(Jonathan Falconer)*

take part in displaying before the public. If there is a 30-day gap then the display itself must be supervised all over again before presenting before the public.

The display programme for the Swordfish and other Flight aircraft, which runs from May to October, is integrated with those of all other Royal Navy display teams. The draft programme for displays is drawn up by Navy Command,

which prioritises and collates bids. The Royal Navy Historic Flight then allocates airframe hours to meet programme requirements, conditioned by the constraint that only 50 hours are available per airframe. Effective allocation of precious airframe hours requires a delicate balance between time spent on display itself with time taken up by practice and training, and both the latter requirements can eat into the 50-hour quota.

Replicating the manning of the Swordfish as it was originally operated presumes the presence of an observer and TAG in the rear cockpit. These crewmembers, like the pilots, are volunteers drawn from front-line or training squadrons. Raising the White Ensign and manning the VGO machine gun are key tasks in flight and ones which give added dramatic impact to the display. The crew in the rear cockpit are also able to wing-fold and, if necessary, start the engine when the aircraft is on the ground.

Where the engine will have to be shut down at an event, a maintainer will accompany the team. This has proved beneficial since (for

RIGHT Maintenance on LS326. The relatively spacious floor area contrasts with the more cramped hangar conditions that would have been experienced by those maintaining Swordfish on aircraft carriers in the Second World War. *(Jonathan Falconer)*

instance) the sparking plugs are notorious for oiling up and in addition to ensuring this does not delay timing of the Royal Navy Historic Flight display, they can assist in ground handling tasks such as folding and spreading wings and engine starting.

Finally, maintenance requirements have to be taken into account, which need their own allocation of time. This is essential time out if the aircraft are to be kept fully airworthy during the display season. While some of the most important tasks are carried out in the hangar during the winter, the ten-hour basic servicing requirement must be fitted in around the display programme and this may be further complicated by pilot availability.

The Royal Navy Historic Flight Swordfish have played a very active part in air show displays over the years, both in the air and in the static park. More important in some ways than exhibiting at air shows are the

ABOVE LS326 at Biggin Hill Air Fair in May 1969. Biggin Hill, the famous Battle of Britain RAF station to the south-east of London has been a favourite venue for air shows since it was released from military use. *(VLR via Keith Wilson)*

LEFT LS326 flies down the crowd line at the Mildenhall air show in June 1987. *(VLR via Keith Wilson)*

ABOVE In May 2013 the Royal Navy Historic Flight made a major contribution to commemorate the 70th anniversary of the 'turning of the tide' in the Battle of the Atlantic. In particular, LS326 performed two important fly-pasts, one along the River Thames and one along the River Mersey. These views were taken from the observer's cockpit as the aircraft proceeded up London's river passing over Canary Wharf [1], past Tower Bridge [2] and finally dropping down to fly alongside HMS *Illustrious* moored at Greenwich [3]. *(RNHF)*

commemorations that they attend. Each year, for example, LS326 or her sister aircraft will overfly the annual FAA TAG service held at the memorial on the seafront at Lee-on-the-Solent, just outside HMS *Daedalus*.

In a recent most fitting tribute, LS326, a veteran

BELOW This is a historic if sad occasion. HMS *Victorious*, the doughty veteran of aerial attacks on the *Bismarck* and Japanese Kamikaze damage among its many actions, is finally bound for the breaker's at Faslane in 1969, some 30 years after she was launched. Accompanying her departure through the waters of Portsmouth Naval Base is LS326. The lone figure standing erect in the rear cockpit of the aircraft saluting the exit of the old lady is Vice-Admiral Sir Richard Janvrin, who had commanded the carrier as Flag Officer Carriers in the mid-1960s. *(The Portsmouth Dockyard Heritage Trust)*

BELOW In with the new. It is 1 July 1985 and the new carrier HMS *Ark Royal* has arrived at Portsmouth Naval Base from Swan Hunters shipyard. She is handed over with due ceremony to the Royal Navy. Alongside a FAA Sea Harrier on the flight deck is LS326, a reminder of the present ship's famous predecessor as well as salutary evidence to *Ark*'s young crew of what a previous generation of FAA personnel had to experience in the course of duty some 40 years before. *(The Portsmouth Dockyard Heritage Trust)*

herself of the Atlantic convoys, played a prominent part in the 2013 commemoration of the Battle of the Atlantic. As part of these celebrations, fly-pasts of HMS *Illustrious* took place at Greenwich and Liverpool to give added and special significance to these important events.

Many and various are the occasions on which the presence of LS326 has been requested. Two examples illustrate the charismatic presence created by the Royal Navy Historic Flight Swordfish. The departure from Portsmouth in 1969 of HMS *Victorious* to the breaker's yard; and the arrival of the new aircraft carrier HMS *Ark Royal V* at the naval base in 1985.

Such occasions perhaps sum up the fundamental raison d'être of the Royal Navy Historic Flight – that is, to maintain a living memorial, a permanent reminder on the ground and in the air, of the contribution made by the men and women of the FAA and its predecessor the Royal Naval Air Service, in war and peace, during more than a century of service to the nation.

Flying and displaying the Fairey Swordfish

Lieutenant Commander Glenn Allison, RN

'The two Royal Navy Historic Flight engineers standing on the port side of the Swordfish aircraft I'm sitting in are winding the handle of the inertia starter with such vigour that the aircraft is literally rocking from side to side. This rocking motion is one of the signs that it is time for me to engage the starter clutch and energise the booster coils inside the cockpit; the other sign is the exhausted cry of "Now!" when they cannot physically wind any more. Woe betide the pilot who has forgotten to put on the magneto switches as there is only just enough stored energy in the starter to turn the engine over about two blades, so if it doesn't start the engineers will have to keep going; an exhausting task.

'Luckily (for me) the engine bursts into life with a few squirts of fuel with the Ki-Gass pump and I quickly set 1,100rpm and make sure the engine keeps running. White smoke is pouring down the starboard side of the aeroplane, choking the assembled crowd behind, but they appear to be enjoying it though. It's the first time I've ever

started the aeroplane myself and I'm about to take her airborne for my second flight, which is a transit from RNAS Yeovilton to Duxford for a static display. My previous sortie was my conversion flight two days earlier with the "Boss", Royal Navy Historic Flight Commanding Officer, Lt Cdr Mike Abbey, MBE, RN.

'Prior to this burst of activity there is a well-practised routine to go through, which ensures all is well to take such an iconic 70-year-old aeroplane into the air. We go through all of the normal flight planning and meteorological briefing at RNAS Yeovilton and arrive at Royal Navy Historic Flight about an hour and a half before launch. At this stage the aeroplane is undergoing Before Flight Servicing (BFS) and the MF700C is signed by the engineers before I sign and take her on charge. All original signatures are removed and the book is safely stowed away in the rear cockpit in true naval fashion.

'The aircraft is always fuelled up to the gunnels – 167½gal. With two crewmembers in the rear cockpit, toolbox, overnight kit, White Ensign (for the display), air bottle rig, the aircraft is still about half-a-ton under its maximum all-up weight (AUW). This full fuel state also gives us about a 300 nautical mile range with enough fuel left for contingency and diversion should we need it. That's about 3½hrs flying!

'As I start to carry out my pilot's walk-round, one of the engineers will begin to fit the four bottom spark plugs to the Bristol Pegasus's cylinders. This is done as late as possible and is a common practice with radial engines to prevent "hydraulicing", a phenomenon that can

BELOW Lt Cdr Glenn Allison, seen alongside a North American Harvard, occasionally on loan to the Royal Navy Historic Flight for training and flight experience purposes. *(Jonathan Falconer)*

ABOVE Post engine start checking for oil leaks.

LEFT The propeller is 'pulled through' by hand until 9 blades have passed through. For each blade passing the 12 o'clock position the pilot pushes the Ki-Gass pump in to prime each cylinder with fuel.

RIGHT The parking brake is applied before start.

ABOVE The throttle is opened slightly and the control column is held firmly against the back stop.

LEFT Ki-Gass hand pump for priming the engine prior to start and for fuelling the engine until the engine driven pump takes over.

BELOW Gang switch for energising the 'booster coil' which enhances the spark in each cylinder helping the engine to start.

FAR LEFT AND LEFT Both magneto switches are selected on before the start sequence begins.

ABOVE When enough energy has been given to the starter flywheel the pilot pulls this toggle to engage the flywheel into the engine.

LEFT While pulling the flywheel toggle the pilot presses down the booster coil with his thumb, while operating the Ki-Gass pump with his right hand. At the same time holding the control column back with a free elbow!

FAR LEFT After start the engine is allowed to warm up to operating temperature.

LEFT Typical fish engine start with lots of smoke from the over-fuelled engine.

FAR LEFT Full power check.

ABOVE Taxying the Swordfish is fairly easy but the air pressure supplying the brakes doesn't last very long, so the short distance out to Yeovilton's Runway 04 is welcome. *(Jonathan Falconer)*

BELOW At 60kts the Swordfish gets herself airborne without me actually doing anything. *(Jonathan Falconer)*

purring at 1,100rpm and warming up slowly, I make myself comfortable and sort out the radios, checking in with ground control and organising my maps. I've taken the advice of other Swordfish pilots and prepared two sets of maps just in case I lose one over the side in flight as has happened on many occasions to other pilots.

'Oil temperature is slow to come up now it's October, so I pull out the oil cooler by-pass and soon see it rise to 15 degrees; the cylinder-head temperature also slowly gets up to the required 100 degrees. I can now run up the engine to check the magneto drop is within limits. To do this I give the wind-up signal to the two engineers hovering at the wingtips and they go aft and put their weight on to the tail-plane struts. This helps to keep the tail down as I bring up the engine to 1,800rpm and the Pegasus sounds amazing as I get buffeted in the cockpit by the slipstream.

'Taxying out to Runway 04 at RNAS Yeovilton is only a few hundred yards, which is convenient as the air pressure supplying the Swordfish's brakes is generated by a compressor driven off the engine and doesn't last very long. As tail-draggers go the Swordfish is fairly easy to taxi; the rear crew can also assist with 'look-out' by leaning out to the sides to see around the engine.

'I run through the checklist ensuring the mixture is set to "Rich" (which will ensure +0.5in of boost is available from the supercharged engine for take-off) and also that the fuel selector is moved from "Gravity" to "Normal/Both". In the "Normal/Both" setting an engine-driven pump will transfer fuel from the main 155gal tank to the 12½gal gravity tank. If the fuel selector is left selected to "Gravity" the fuel will last about 20mins before the tank is drained, so it's quite an important check! Once lined up, I wind up the Pegasus to 1,500rpm. This ensures there is ample rudder control as I release the brakes and start rolling.

'The sensations in this aircraft are different to any I have experienced before, and my flight in the rear cockpit with the Boss prepared me well before giving it a go myself. After observing the Boss's sortie, listening intently to his commentary and words of wisdom, I felt fully confident of launching on my first sortie,

severely damage an engine due to oil pooling in the top of the cylinders. I give the aircraft a very thorough look-over checking the plugs are in, attachments of the landing wires and flying wires, wing-fold mechanisms, exposed control cables, undercarriage and the rear and front cockpits. Once in the cockpit I go through the initial checks and pre-start drill and indicate to the engineers I am ready to prime the engine, which requires them to pull each prop through while I squirt in fuel using the Ki-Gass pump.

'Sitting in the cockpit with the engine now

with him now standing bravely in the observer's position in the back.

'The sortie began with some medium and steep turns, before stalling, clean, in the turn and finally with the ailerons fully drooped. Wingovers were also practised ready for display flying before returning to the circuit for normal and glide approaches. On that first flight I found that the aircraft was very forgiving indeed and refused to drop a wing in the stall unless grossly mishandled. The signs of the approaching stall are given by the aerodynamic slats deploying, normally independently and with a noticeable 'thump'! The attitude is not particularly nose-up and there is hardly any buffet to speak of; at this stage the stick is pulled as far back as it will go into one's stomach. As the aircraft enters the stall there is a slight nose drop, which seems to prevent the aircraft going any deeper into the stall. This all occurs at around 48 to 50kt. I tried it again with the ailerons fully drooped and found the aircraft extremely heavy in roll with almost two hands required on the control column; the stalling speed was reduced by a couple of knots but nothing too significant.

'Having done a fair bit of training in the Royal Navy Historic Flight Chipmunk and a privately owned Percival Provost I was keen to get into the circuit and practise landing the aircraft. I was struck at how much the aircraft sinks when the pilot retards the throttle; the Swordfish generates a hell of a lot of drag.

'I turned "Final" in the same place as my previous Chipmunk training circuit, setting about 1,300rpm and aimed for a slightly shallow approach – "wheeling" the Swordfish on in a tail-low attitude seems to work fine. I learned on these first few circuits not to cut the power too quickly, as any rate of descent leads to a bounce off the springy undercarriage; it's far better to leave a trickle of power on if you have the luxury of a nice long runway.

'Today, two days later, as I sit in the cockpit on the threshold of Runway 04, I am now a fully fledged Royal Navy Swordfish pilot with 45min P1 in my logbook.

'After gaining clearance from Tower I increase power to static boost and immediately there is a fantastic amount of noise and incredible amount of slipstream, blocking out all intercom and radio transmissions. It seems an age before the Swordfish starts on her way down the runway, 7,600lb of metal and fabric (and three people) slowly gains airspeed before I start to raise the tail with a huge push forward on the spade-type control column. I was prepared for a bit of swing, but it's hardly noticeable; the Swordfish is now up to 60kt and she gets herself airborne without me actually doing anything.

'I glance down at the oil pressure, which is indicating a solid 60psi, the airspeed is accelerating up to 80kt now and I haul back on the control column a little more and trim her for the climb. The noise is still incredible along with the buffeting on my military-issue flying helmet, causing annoying reverberations (oh, for a leather helmet) and communicating with anyone at this stage would be impossible.

'As we pass 800ft I throttle back a little just so I can turn on my microphone and make a radio call to Tower and chop across to Yeovilton Approach. I also need to select the mixture to "Altitude" and ensure the gravity fuel tank is still full. To check the gravity tank I have to turn on a light switch and look through a slot; the gauge is on top of the fuel tank behind the instrument panel and slightly difficult to see.

'After levelling off at 1,500ft the noise levels subside a little and I can start to communicate with the rear crew as I set up the aircraft to cruise at 90kt. The boost gauge indicates minus 3in now and the rpm is steady at 1,900. I'm also watching the oil pressure and temperature like a hawk as I can see oil on the starboard interplane struts; the Boss assures me this is fairly normal and is usually kicked out during the start – phew!

'The day is not too blustery but even at 1,500ft I can feel the aircraft gently being affected by updraughts and downdraughts; on looking at the huge wings I can also see them flexing up and down. The engine valves can be seen rapidly opening and closing as I look past the Pegasus, which is slightly strange at first!

'During the transit to Duxford I get into a routine and complete "FEEL" checks every 10min, remembering to re-synchronise the Direction Indicator from the P11 compass, (mounted upside down in front of the pilot and hence read using a mirror). Radio calls are made to maintain a traffic service wherever possible; I find that communication works best

if I lower my seat fully so my head is out of the slipstream, simultaneously retarding the throttle to reduce engine noise. I'm also keen to talk to as many airfields as possible, hoping they will invite me to fly through, which most do – I also like hearing my own call-sign "Navy Swordfish" being repeated back.

'It's a beautiful autumn day and we are now flying along at 1,000ft into a fairly strong wind, so I'm trying to maximise the ground speed without compromising my options if the engine were to stop. I practised a couple of glide approaches with the Boss in the back and I was surprised that the Swordfish with its huge wing area glides so poorly, almost like a brick to be precise! The large fixed pitch propeller actually gives a lot of drag.

'I make a radio call to Duxford and I'm told that a B-17 has just got airborne off Runway 06, the show is about to start and I am cleared for a straight-in approach. "Would I like the grass or the hard?" they ask. Oh and it's great to see us back after so long! I ask the Boss what he thinks my best option would be. He replies that the crowd will see us better if we land on the grass runway and it's all about them after all. I therefore line up for a straight-in approach to Duxford's Runway 06 Grass and can see the B-17 and a couple of "little friends" (Mustangs) orbiting to the north, waiting to open the air show.

'At this point the 70kt approach seems awfully slow, but I resist the temptation to come barrelling in too fast. After all I don't want to

announce the Swordfish's arrival back on the display circuit with an embarrassing bounce or go-around. The landing was almost perfect by some fluke; I could feel the main wheels settle on to the grass as we decelerated. A little bump gently launched us airborne for a few more yards before the Swordfish returned to the ground in the three-point attitude.

'The Swordfish is a delight to fly and providing the pilot has gained some tail-dragger experience it's a reasonably easy transition to make. One of the striking things about the Swordfish is its size and the pilot sits up at around 15ft, slightly higher than the Chipmunk. This takes a little getting used to but not long before the eye is calibrated to the new round-out height.

'As I turned off the runway to head to a parking slot I was now aware of the huge crowd of some 15,000 people. The White Ensign was put up in the observer's cockpit and we enthusiastically returned the excited waves from everyone as we taxied in to our allocated spot in front of the historic control tower. There ended my second flight in the Swordfish.

'I was absolutely elated and literally flying high. After shutting down and climbing out to meet our Royal Navy Historic Flight engineer, who had driven up as advance party, I then realised I was actually quite exhausted from the flight, which had only lasted about 1hr 30min, due mainly to the fact that you get quite a battering from the slipstream. The aeroplane constantly needs trimming as the centre of gravity and drag changes as the rear crew move around in the slipstream. Anyway, as you can imagine I got no sympathy from anyone, particularly from our engineer who handed me a rag and ordered me to start wiping off oil from the starboard side. I couldn't really argue as I had just enjoyed the most amazing experience for the last few hours, flying a legendary Royal Navy aircraft.

'Since that second flight, which was back in 2010, I've been very lucky to display the aircraft around the UK enjoying some fantastic flying experiences into the bargain. One of the most memorable sorties was displaying at the Dartmouth Regatta where the obvious routing to come "on slot" is to fly down the River Dart, fairly low under the gaze of the Britannia Royal Naval College. Taking the aircraft up to Edinburgh for a display at East Fortune involved a very long transit and included flying up the River Mersey and past some very famous landmarks. Liverpool is so important to the Royal Navy and played a major role in the Battle of the Atlantic 70 years ago. After departing Liverpool, the transit took me and my crew up the west coast, taking in the Lake District and the lowlands of Scotland. There were some real 'pinch me' moments on that trip and the weather was very kind.

'Finally, as a legendary Royal Navy aircraft Swordfish LS326 is much in demand and I was

also recently asked to give the Duke of York, who served in the Royal Navy as a helicopter pilot, his first flight in a Swordfish, which was a real privilege.

'The Royal Navy and the Royal Navy Historic Flight are committed to keeping the Swordfish serviceable for future generations to be able to see her flying, rather than in a museum, where she can best serve our aim to act as a living memorial to all those who have served in the FAA and the Royal Naval Air Service through two world wars and many other conflicts.'

ABOVE Nothing unusual in a little oil leak! In fact a common feature of good British machinery! *(Jonathan Falconer)*

FAR LEFT LS326 trailed by three Royal Navy helicopters during the 2013 Battle of the Atlantic event. Note the prominent mass of Liverpool's Anglican Cathedral just visible beyond the port elevator. *(RNHF)*

LEFT With the broad sunlit sweep of the River Mersey estuary behind her, LS326 overflies a much welcomed landfall for many a crew of an Atlantic convoy merchant ship or its naval escort. *(RNHF)*

Chapter Seven

Operating the Swordfish

The word 'unforgettable' sums up the response of those who have flown the 'white lady of the skies'. Second World War Fleet Air Arm veterans and Royal Navy Historic Flight aircrew alike testify to her gentle but positive flight characteristics and old fashioned charm as she sails serenely above the landscape.

OPPOSITE Swordfish LS326 over Portsmouth dockyard on **14 November 2010.** *(Lee Howard)*

Wartime experiences

To achieve a proper understanding of the significance of a historic aircraft it is necessary to retrace one's steps and examine the context in which it served. What was it like to fly during its FAA and RAF service? To what exigencies were the wartime Swordfish and its crew subject? How was it viewed by those who flew and maintained it?

The vicissitudes of striking off charge and storage with possibly consequent neglect, together with subsequent minor modifications and upgradings, will have taken their toll in eroding a machine's authenticity, where it is of the Swordfish's vintage. Therefore reliving the experiences of those involved with it in service can provide valuable clues to its character and features.

We are fortunate that many detailed accounts exist which describe the trials, tribulations and triumphs of the Stringbag men during the momentous years of the Second World War. As well as highlighting the aircraft's characteristics and foibles, these accounts highlight the attitudes of men towards their machine.

In-flight behaviour

John Moffat, of *Bismarck* fame, made his first acquaintance with the Swordfish when undertaking TSR training at HMS *Sanderling* near Glasgow. This was a shore establishment that later became Glasgow Airport. Full of praise for its good weight-lifting capabilities, the result he felt of its generous wing area, he nevertheless initially viewed its flying characteristics less enthusiastically. 'I felt that I was riding a carthorse instead of a steeplechaser at first, but the more I flew it, the more I began to appreciate its qualities.'

Its ability to shrug off attacking enemy fighters was well known. John Moffat confirms this capability, describing the 180-degree turns the machine would make at sea level in such circumstances: 'The Swordfish had a much smaller turning circle than any fast fighter, and moreover it had such an advantageous lift ratio that you could reduce its speed to just 70kt in the turn and it would continue on a perfect line. Most planes need more power to complete a turn but not the Swordfish.'[1]

Charles Lamb of 815 NAS, training on the Swordfish early in the war at HMS *Kestrel*, Worthy Down, Hampshire, commended its docility:

'The Stringbag could be very roughly handled in incredible attitudes without stalling, providing the pilot knew what he was doing. To stall a Swordfish by mistake was almost an impossibility. Marc Lobelle (Fairey's designer) had given the aircraft a stalling speed of 55kt and no pilot however ham-handed could allow his speed to drop to that extent without noticing. To induce it into a spin was quite hard work; the aircraft could be stood on its tail in mid-flight so that it became almost stationary, before it would drop into a stalled turn, and then recovery could be instantaneous. Quick application of throttle and opposite rudder and a speedy lowering of the nose would provide almost immediate stability when the manoeuvre could be repeated without fear.'[2]

The famed naval test pilot **Eric 'Winkle' Brown** with probably the widest experience of all Second World War types, was equally complimentary:

'In cruising flight at 85kt the Swordfish was very stable about all axes and was very easy to fly on instruments, but harmony of control was somewhat spoiled by oversensitivity of rudder, although this cancelled itself out in aiding the slightly heavy ailerons in endowing this ungainly looking aircraft with an agility totally out of keeping with its appearance and its rate of turn was phenomenal.

'... the aircraft was undeniably vice-less and liberties could be taken that would have guaranteed any other aircraft stalling and spinning long before. The rudder bias was somewhat inadequate in a power-off glide, but a normal landing was ridiculously easy. With mixture set "RICH", carburettor intake set "COLD" and brakes checked "OFF", the Swordfish would virtually land itself. This was normally effected without flap at 70kt on an airfield and at 60kts on a carrier.'[3]

Eric Brown goes on to explain that flap (a symmetrical 8-degree aileron droop) was only used for catapulting. In carrier landing this was not advocated since the aircraft, with flap selected, might float over the arrester wires.

Donald Payne describes his first solo in a Swordfish, undertaken at No 9 Advanced Flying Unit (AFU) at Findo Gask near Perth:

'I found myself airborne before I was halfway down the runway ... she seemed amazingly simple to fly: there was no need to bother about things like flaps and undercarriage ... right from the start I felt at ease in the Swordfish. She was also a wonderfully forgiving aircraft, and in all the time I flew her I always had the feeling that if I did something wrong she would simply give a sigh of resignation and keep flying straight and level.

'In the first half of the war most pilots who flew a Swordfish Mark I were enthusiastic about its handling characteristics and performance – apart, obviously, from its speed. It was reliable, adaptable, responsive, amazingly manoeuvrable and quite simply fun to fly. ... In the second half of the war, however, the Swordfish Mark I was progressively superseded by the Swordfish II and then the III, the last so burdened with weaponry (for example, the Oscar acoustic torpedo) and equipment (such as ASV radar) that its performance deteriorated. Its top speed was reduced from 120 to 90kt and it lost much of its manoeuvrability.

'Swordfish were dependable; and indeed for an aircraft expected to fly long distances in all weathers over the sea, dependability was perhaps the quality that was most important.

'They had superb handling characteristics and their short take-off run, their low landing speed and their stability and responsiveness – even when close to stalling – enabled them to operate from carriers in conditions in which no other aircraft could be airborne.'[4]

LEFT Captain Eric 'Winkle' Brown is possibly the best known, and certainly the most experienced of all the doughty band of Fleet Air Arm pilots. Both while serving on wartime carriers and then as a naval test pilot, he earned a reputation as an aviator par excellence. Among his many achievements was the first ever landing-on of a jet aircraft when he piloted a Vampire on to the flight deck of HMS *Ocean*, and a similar world first when he successfully put down on a carrier in a twin-engined Sea Mosquito. *(RNHF)*

Stanley Brand: 'The Fairey Swordfish Mark I and her younger sibling the Blackburn Swordfish Mark II were stalwart, docile, reliable, slow, sturdy, and uncomplicated, which together outweighed the draughts, noise and lack of urinal facilities.

'However, nothing could quite compensate for the lack of heating circuits for gloves and Irvin suits except a tropical appointment. These "Stringbags" had Bristol Pegasus XXX engines, which would continue to run, in my own experience, even after losing a cylinder head, though of course, for a limited time. They could be fitted with a fixed fine pitch propeller to give extra power to carry an extra load or reduce take-off run at the expense of high revving wear and tear and increased petrol consumption. They would continue to fly after losing enormous amounts of wing and control surface fabric through fire or gunfire and would respond to the controls even on the point of stall.

'They could turn more tightly than any other Allied front-line plane and could side-slip out of a difficult spot. The Swordfish undercarriage could withstand a heavy landing, which would leave a lesser aircraft immobile on deck with its wheel struts pushed up through its wings.'[5]

Take-off and landing

Nimble though the Swordfish was normally, 'weighed down to the gunnels' with stores in true Stringbag fashion there were occasions when take-offs were touch and go.

Nat Gould remembered such occasions. When based on Malta and serving with 830 NAS, he and his crew were tasked with night sorties from Hal Far airfield:

'When ready for take-off we taxied to the beginning of the single dim flare path lights – these were flashed on for a while then switched off because Jerry often waited overhead to drop anti-personnel bombs. The pilot had to memorise the flare path position then let the Swordfish roll into the darkness, inevitably struggling to take off as we could only take off down 'drome regardless of which way the wind blew. We might be carrying a crew of two, a full overload petrol tank in the observer's cockpit and either bombs, torpedoes or magnetic mines. The weight was considerable, but with the odd exception we just managed to clear the stone wall at the end of the

'drome and make our rendezvous around Fifla Rock and then form into a tight vee formation to set off on our operation.'[6]

Landings

Flying off HMS *Courageous* in September 1939 **Charles Lamb** experienced the classic dilemma of the naval aviator, running short of fuel with no sign of his carrier – in this case flying some 500 miles west of Land's End. Once he had located *Courageous* it became a race to gain the arrester wires before the engine stopped in a one-and-only chance of landing on. He describes the final tense moments:

'While the ship is turning, the wind across the flight deck can be violently antagonistic to a pilot who tries to land before the turn is completed. Since we were about to run out of petrol the turn seemed interminable and after one half-circuit of the ship I decided to risk the crosswind and the violent turning motion and get down before it was too late.

'At this point seeing the Swordfish taking up a final approach, the batsman frantically signalled a wave-off: he could not know that the petrol indicator had been showing "E" for the last 10min at least. The Swordfish has a Bristol Pegasus IIIM3 radial engine, which obscures the flight deck and the ship in the very last stages of a deck landing. Normally, by approaching in a gentle turn to port, right down to the deck, it is possible to keep the deck in sight until straightening up; then it is necessary to look between the engine cylinders, at 11 and 12 o'clock, when the yellow bats come into view for a split second as the deck swoops upwards at an alarming rate. This is fine by day but at night the cylinders are always red-hot and glow very brightly, and they can obscure the batsman's illuminated signals altogether.

'That afternoon he (the batsman) was being very helpful – by waving his bats around his head in a frenzied "go round again" sign, and I could see him all the way down to the deck. ... He had every right to wave me off. Apart from the obvious danger of landing on a restricted area, which was swinging violently to starboard as the bow swung to port, I was much too high. In case my petrol gave out in the last few vital seconds, I had kept my height, to remain within the gliding distance all the way down, intending to side-slip if necessary; or to ease the aircraft on to the deck in a stall by opening the throttle with the last few pints of petrol, once we were over the round-down. This is quite an effective method of landing a Swordfish and is known as "hanging on the prop".

'The Swordfish has a strong fixed undercarriage, an enormous rudder and very good brakes. If our landing was rather like that of a clumsy seagull alighting on water in a rush, it was nevertheless successful and nothing broke. The hook picked up a wire and all was well.'[7]

There followed one of the great ironies of Charles Lamb's war. His was to be the very last landing ever on *Courageous*. At the moment he and his crew stepped into the wardroom the carrier was dealt a death blow. It was hit by two U-boat torpedoes.

John Galbraith of 836 NAS was the pilot of Swordfish LS320 embarked on the MAC ship *Empire McCrae*. During escort duties with Convoy HX274 his Swordfish was launched for a patrol. No sooner had the aircraft taken off than the storm increased to Force 10 with a resultant reduction in visibility, not to mention untenable flying conditions. The sortie was aborted. The story was taken up by a young RCN corvette captain, whose ship was acting as plane guard:

'The Stringbag flew low overhead, with the aircrew waving from their cockpits, seemingly quite unconcerned, but I wondered how they could ever be recovered in that howling gale. We were very close to the carrier and could hardly believe what we saw next. The carrier steamed into wind, as did the Swordfish (which made her ground speed about zero), and the carrier came up under the aircraft from behind and took her on board over the bows! Men leapt on the aircraft as soon as she touched down and she was recovered without damage or injury.'[8]

Together with MAC ships, Escort Carriers bore the brunt of convoy protection, operating with their NAS within the Arctic Circle to Russia as well as shepherding vital supplies across the North Atlantic and guarding convoys down to Gibraltar.

N. Smith gives a vivid account of Swordfish operations from HMS *Tracker* late in 1943.

'The beginning of November saw SW gales battering the ship and its aircraft. It is clear

ABOVE Swordfish 'C' takes off from HMS *Biter*. Embarked with the Swordfish of 824 NAS *Biter* escorted a total of 16 Atlantic and Gibraltar convoys during 1943 and 1944. Her aircraft achieved two shared U-boat sinkings. A most unusual claim to fame for *Biter* lies in the fact that damage was caused on one occasion by a torpedo from one of her own Swordfish. Her rudder was struck by the weapon after the aircraft in question ditched close to the ship. Note the ship's disruptive camouflage scheme. *(FAA Museum)*

BELOW The view over the tail of a Swordfish of HMS *Biter* and ships of the convoy she was guarding, March 1944. The wake of the Escort Carrier clearly indicates that the ship has turned into wind and out of line to facilitate the take-off of its aircraft. *(IWM A22716)*

ABOVE This Swordfish appears to have swung violently and entered into an argument with the Escort Carrier's bridge, resulting in the disintegration of the whole of the starboard wing assembly. With limited space and repair resources and the need to resume operations, damage of this magnitude might result in the remainder of the aircraft being dumped overboard after saving selected parts for spares. *(FAA Museum)*

aircrew feared the worst as they clambered aboard their machines ... they knew perfectly well that even if the weather allowed them to take off it might have changed for the worst by the time they wanted to land on. And the take-off was no picnic. Crowds lined the catwalk to see the show, very much in the mood and spirit of a speedway crowd. It is a fact that every one of those spectators made sure he had somewhere to dive if the ship or the plane should stage a surprise move.

'Here she comes. Commander Flying has given the affirmative. Ship steady into the wind and sea. Louder roar. Past the bridge. Up, up, yes she's airborne ... did you see that dip, just missed the 40 millimetres.

'Watch out, C for Charlie's landing on. Bats is doing his stuff. Down port, steady now. Down starboard. Ship's gone very quiet. Lower now. Here she comes, down, down. This is going to be a lovely three-point. Right cut.

'The dirty ... ship suddenly dropped her stern then. 25ft. Poor old Stringbag dropped like a stone and spread-eagled her undercarriage. Prang No 3. Fall in Maintenance. Another night's work. She must be up tomorrow.'[9]

Evidence of the limited landing run available to pilots landing on Escort Carriers is reflected in the many overshoot experiences.

Stanley Yeo described an occasion in the Clyde. HMS *Dasher*, the tragic subject of an explosion in March 1943, was working up its 837 NAS aircrew. While acting as the observer, his pilot brought the Swordfish in to land on the carrier. All four arrester wires were missed:

'My pilot broke all the rules concerning deck landings. He missed all four arrester wires and instead of going into the crash barrier he opened

up the engine to full throttle, yanked the stick back and just staggered over the crash barrier, very close to stalling speed. It so happened that the ship's photographer got a perfect shot of this incident, showing the arrester hook just 6in above the crash barrier.'[10]

Wallace Giddings, a petty officer with 886 NAS on HMS *Attacker*, recalls a spectator's view of take-offs and landings-on:

'I remember the lads hanging on to the tail of a Swordfish while the engine was revved up before take-off, hats and bits and pieces being blown over the side. When they approached the deck for landing, they seemed to me to hover like a seagull hanging in flight looking for food. "Bats" would be standing out there on the edge of the flight deck with a yellow bat in each hand guiding it down on to the deck – a most hazardous job, I used to think. I recall occasions when he laid flat on the deck as the kite was too near as it roared on. Then came the thump as the hook caught and the plane was safely on the deck. I was in the catwalk expecting an almighty crash, when the famous photograph was taken of one of our Swordfish just missing the barrier and being waved round again.'[11]

Operating the Swordfish

Instructions and advice on flying the Swordfish was contained in wartime Pilot's Notes. Such information undoubtedly took account of the exigencies of war. In addition, service during the Second World War with Naval Air Squadrons from the Arctic Circle to the Indian Ocean meant that the content of Air Publications needed to take into account the wide range of conditions in which the Swordfish would be operating. Not least the temperature and humidity factors postulated by such service.

What follows is a summary of checks and instructions that are principally based on material from Air Publication AP101B, which has been specially prepared by the Handling Squadron, Yeovilton, to assist members of the Royal Navy Historic Flight in the handling of their two airworthy Swordfish aircraft, LS326 and W5856. In addition, brief notes are provided that give the opinions of pilots with experience of the type (Brown, Payne and Allison).

On entering the cockpit the following checks are to be carried out:

- Both ignition switches to be OFF.
- The battery master to be OFF.
- Fuel cock to be OFF.
- Brakes to be OFF.

Then the following checks are to be carried out externally, working clockwise round the aircraft from the port wingtip:

- The air charging pin to be in and secure.*
- The cover to the pressure head to have been removed and for it to be in good condition.
- The wing locks to be secure with their catches on and their safety pins in.* The top red indicator must be flush with the wing surface.
- The condition of the tyres should be checked with special attention to the security of the hub bolt.
- Moving round the aircraft each of the landing and flying wires should be checked at attachments, for tension and for their general condition.
- Check exposed control cables.
- Any engine oil leaks must be identified if these have occurred. Installation of all four lower-most plugs to be confirmed. [Plugs will have been removed to prevent the build-up of oil in the bottom cylinders, which in turn causes hydraulic lock and possible damage to the engine.]
- Propeller checks. Visual check of condition with propeller turned through two complete revolutions [ie six blade passes] if first flight of the day.
- Checks to be made of all intakes and the oil cooler to confirm these are clear of obstructions.

Further cockpit checks

Flying controls including the elevator trim are to be full and free with rudder bias set half down.

- Battery master and brakes to be 'ON'.
- Pitot heating, radio and external lights all to be 'OFF'.
- Throttle and mixture controls to be full and free. Mixture to be set at 'ALT'.

- Oil cooler, bypass and carburettor intake to be closed.
- Lights to boost coil, compass, fire extinguisher and map light dimmer to be 'OFF'.
- Generator warning, fuel gauge and fuel low pressure warning lights to be 'ON'.
- Priming pump to be unhoused, fuel cock to be set to 'MAIN ONLY' and fuel hand pump to be unscrewed.
- Boost gauge, CHT and oil temperature gauge readings should be noted.
- Check booster coils, identification lights, transponder and wireless are all 'OFF'.
- Check brake air accumulator 160psi and 80/80 with brakes 'ON'.
- Set and wind clock. Set instruments to zero as necessary.
- Adjust friction on harness release.

Engine start-up

- Fuel to be at 'MAIN ONLY'.
- Throttle to be closed.
- Brakes 'ON' at required and equal pressure.
- Both ignition switches to be at 'OFF'.
- First push the Ki-Gass priming pump one stroke. (If engine not operated recently more strokes may be necessary. Until resistance is felt.)
- Report 'Ready to prime 1 IN' to groundcrew.

The ground crew will then pull the propeller through for nine blades. As a blade passes through the 12 o'clock position the pilot pushes the Ki-Gass priming pump one stroke to ensure each of the nine cylinders is primed with fuel for the engine start.

- Set throttle open ½in.
- Both ignition switches to be 'ON'.
- Both booster coils to be 'ON'.
- Signal 'Ready to start' to groundcrew.
- When inertia starter is at maximum speed (indicated by sideways movement of aircraft) the groundcrew call 'NOW'.
- Then press 'ON' and hold booster coil gang switch and pull and hold inertia starter switch.

* RNHF modification

- Operate Ki-Gass priming pump again until the engine is running then release clutch and booster start switch.
- When engine is running smoothly do dead cut check.
- Instruments to be checked at this point:
- Oil pressure: rising to 60psi.
- Brake pressures: 160psi and 80/80.
- Power: set throttle to give 1,100rpm.
- Fuel to be on 'GRAVITY'.
- Priming pump to be housed.
- Booster coils to be 'OFF' with lights out.

Engine run-up checks
- Check tail held down by aircrew.
- Mixture to be at 'ALT'.
- Throttle set to give 1,800rpm.
- Switch off alternate magnetos. Drop to be 50 with maximum of 75.
- Retard the throttle to fully closed and check idling at 650–700rpm.
- Select fuel to be 'NORMAL BOTH'. Check fuel levels.
- Oil cooler to be closed.
- CHT to be more than 100 degrees C.
- Oil temperature to be more than 15 degrees C.

RIGHT The pilot's cockpit showing instrument panel, control column, windscreen, flap control wheel and rocking head assembly.
(Jonathan Falconer)

Pre take-off checks
- Flaps 'UP'. Elevator 2 divisions nose down with the rudder. Controls generally full and free.
- Mixture to be 'RICH' with setting of throttle friction as required.
- Oil cooler to be closed. Check oil temperature and pressure OK.
- Check gravity tank full and select 'NORMAL BOTH'.
- Instruments erect and synchronised.
- Harnesses secure and locked.

Taxying
- Need to zigzag because of blocked view, but rear crew may assist with their better sideways view.
- Aircraft has tendency to 'weathercock' in high winds.
- Air pressure in air bottle is limited so minimum use of brakes if possible.

Take-off/cruising/landing notes
(From the experience of Messrs Brown, Payne and Allison.)

- Generally a short take-off distance.
- At take-off, throttle to be opened slowly with +2lb boost to 1,500 to 2,000rpm, giving ample rudder control.
- Swing to be counteracted with rudder.
- Climb away speed around 70kt when boost can be reduced to +½lb boost.
- Safely airborne, mixture can be set to 'ALT'. Check fuel is on 'NORMAL BOTH'. (The fuel pump at this stage is transferring fuel from the main 155gal tank to the 12½gal gravity tank and onwards to the engine.)
- Typical cruising speed at normal altitude will be 85–90kt.
- Rate of climb at, say, 7,000lb take-off weight, will be approximately 1,000ft/min.
- Landing with engine revs at around 1,300rpm and a shallow approach. While the aircraft has a tendency to sink with a reduction of throttle, it is best to leave a small amount of power on just before touch-down so as to avoid the tendency of the aircraft to 'bounce'.

Deck landing, the DCLO and batting

From the very first pioneering deck landings of Squadron Commander Dunning on HMS *Furious* in August 1917, it became clear that the oncoming pilot would require guidance from the ship (later carrier) if landings-on were to be safely and effectively executed and accidents thereby avoided. By the time of the entry of the Fairey Swordfish into Royal Navy service in the 1930s, effective procedures were in place in the FAA, which in the main achieved that aim.

From that time until the introduction of the pioneering automated mirror systems in the 1970s, the Deck Landing Control Officer (DLCO) aka 'Batsman', was to prove to be the key player in all carrier deck landings. His signals to the oncoming pilot were critical.

As with all other naval aviation activities the process was subject to naval discipline. Eventually the signals conveyed to the pilot were to become instructions rather than advice, orders rather than recommendations. As such, failure to respond to them could result in courts martial procedures.

Having noted that his carrier had turned into wind the naval pilot would make his final approach downwind of the ship on its port side. The DCLO's commands would commence

1–5 The landing-on approach of a Swordfish. The Batsman or Deck Control Landing Officer (DCLO) is signalling instructions to the pilot. The position of the bats reflects the extent to which speed, height and attitude are right for a good touch-down and engagement with the arrester wires. The final cross hands signal is for the engine to be 'cut'. *(FAA Museum)*

6 – 'M2-C' catches the wire as it lands aboard HMS *Argus*. Apart from a brief period in the Mediterranean *Argus* was employed as a training and trials carrier in home waters. This photo could have been taken during the former period of duty. *(Copyright unknown)*

ABOVE A Swordfish appears to have over-run the arrester wires and has been halted by the crash barrier. Deck crew are hurriedly working to move the errant aircraft out of the way of further landings-on. *(FAA Museum)*

BELOW Bats. These are the signals used by the DCLO responsible for guiding incoming aircraft in to safe deck landings. *(Roy Scorer)*

■ STEADY GO UP
■ GO DOWN GO STARBOARD
■ GO PORT SLOW DOWN
■ GO DOWN MORE POWER
■ WAVE OFF CUT ENGINE

at the point where the incoming aircraft had completed its turn into wind and had levelled up for the final stages of descent and landing.

From this point onwards the speed and attitude of the aircraft would be critical factors in making an effective landing. The following sequence illustrates the meaning of the signals made by the DCLO with his bats. It must be remembered that the final touchdown position of the aircraft along the flight deck was another critical factor, particularly when it is borne in mind that the aircraft's arrester hook must engage in an early set of the transverse arrester wires already raised on deck.

STEADY   SLOW DOWN   GO DOWN   MORE POWER

GO UP   WAVE OFF   GO PORT   GO STARBOARD   CUT ENGINE

The art of landing-on involved dedicated practice. Initial trial landings were undertaken on shore. The facility for this was known as ADDL. For this to be carried out Naval Air Stations such as those at Macrihanish in Scotland and Henstridge in Somerset were equipped with 'dummy flight decks'. This involved marking out a short section of main runway so that it resembled the dimensions of a flight deck, often complete with arrester gear. Trainee naval pilots would be able to get used to the limited landing run of the flight deck and the need for precise control of attitude, speed and power.

It should be borne in mind that the flight deck dimensions of the smallest carriers, the grain carrier conversion MAC ships, were of the order of 400ft long by 60ft wide, the latter dimension allowing just 6ft latitude each side of a landing Swordfish.

Deck handling and ranging

With its biplane configuration and with a 45ft 6in span and a length of just over 36ft the Swordfish was a bulky aircraft to manoeuvre. Depending on the mission a number of aircraft, perhaps up to squadron strength, might have to be ranged on the flight deck. In those circumstances Swordfish with their relatively large spans could only be ranged with wings staggered. For start-up purposes space would need to be opened up between the individual machines.

It can be seen that such crowded conditions called for the exercise of considerable handling skills. Add to that factor an ever present sea and wind state and one can appreciate the difficulties that were faced by those entrusted with positioning an aircraft on a carrier.

All but the tanker form of MAC ship were equipped with hangars. A flying programme would thus start with the Swordfish being individually pushed/pulled by the handling party from its position in the hangar, possibly after release from lashings, along to the lift to be taken up to the flight deck. Hangar stowage required wings to be fully folded. Therefore, once propelled by manpower to its position either ranged or in the flying off position, the wings would be unfolded, with the critical red-painted locking levers and red button-type safety indicators all checked.

If as would be the case with Escort Carriers, a full flight might require to be airborne, those aircraft waiting to be called forward would be ranged at the rear end of the flight deck.

Each engine would be started in turn with two members of the deck party operating the inertia handle while two further members would lie on deck by the chocks. Run-up tests required further assistance in holding down the tailplane. Only on removal of the two wheel chocks would the aircraft's brakes come into

operation since the limited pneumatic capacity of the reservoir required careful conservation.

With a crowded rear flight deck, particularly as experienced in the large Fleet Carriers, conditions varied from the dangerous to that of considerable peril. Individuals in the deck handling party in among the aircraft, faced whirring airscrews and powerful slipstreams with the added threats of pitching seas and crosswinds. Aircrew also faced considerable discomfort and risk when getting to their

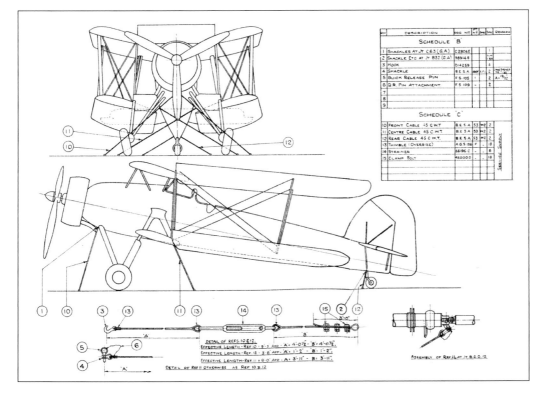

aircraft. The observer in particular weighed down with additional equipment including the famous Bigsworth Board, had to make his way past and through the windswept space, before climbing aboard.

Summing up the Swordfish

Wartime experiences, especially in the extreme conditions in which the Swordfish had to operate on Atlantic and Arctic convoys in the Second World War, serve to provide it with an enviable record. All those who piloted or crewed it during those momentous times testify to a combination of ruggedness, reliability and docile handling hardly equalled by any other of its contemporaries.

Those individuals of the Royal Navy Historic Flight lucky enough to be entrusted with displaying their two flying examples are able to draw inspiration from the wealth of Swordfish memories still vividly etched in the minds of veteran pilots and aircrew who are fortunately still with us.

From recollections and from present-day flying experiences it is possible to draw together some conclusions about Swordfish behaviour and, inevitably, the constraints, which apply as much now as they did 70 years ago.

First the question of handling. There is no doubt that the aircraft has a docility second to none for its type and period. Its design represented the final bowing out of the biplane era.

Generous wing area giving low wing loading and a specification for calling for range and endurance rather than speed, combined to endow the Swordfish with qualities that still appeal to the pilot. Undoubtedly the deck landing and take-off requirement ensured a well-behaved response to controls during these critical manoeuvres.

For all its qualities, however, the Swordfish design in operational terms had its drawbacks, or to be more charitable, idiosyncrasies. Fuel supply is a problem. The system of fuel feed, via what is in effect a header tank, presumes vigilance in checking fuel state. This worry is compounded by the crude nature of the gauge, viewed as it is through a small eye-level aperture, ahead of the pilot.

Visibility is another area in which problems have always been experienced. By their nature large radial engines represented a major incursion into sight lines, as compared with an in-line equivalent. While seated high above the thrust line the Swordfish pilot nevertheless contended with an obscured view that was particularly critical in the final approach stage of carrier landings. However, the Swordfish was not alone in this respect.

Discomfort looms large in the reminiscences of Swordfish aircrew. Draughty, noisy and generally uncomfortable is the consensus view of all those who sailed in her. This clearly was a major factor influencing the design of its presumed successor the Fairey Albacore connection with its enclosed integrally heated cabins. There is little doubt that the degree of exposure experienced by the aircrew required fortitude on their part that only the Royal Navy could supply. There is, however, one slight caveat or qualification regarding this factor. That is the residual concern, dating from the early days of flying, that closed cockpits, despite their increased comfort margins, did nevertheless represent a reduction in visibility; especially so given the tendency for the misting up of canopies.

Finally mention must be made, when addressing concerns for comfort, of the totally inadequate provision for in-flight urination. Complained of by many and especially critical when one bears in mind the length of flying time and the cold latitudes in which operations took place.

The Swordfish was an amazing aircraft with almost magical qualities and one which gained a place in the affections of those who flew in her that was achieved by no other 20th-century aircraft design.

Source notes:

1. Moffat, John, *I Sank the Bismarck* (Bantam Press, 2009)
2. Lamb, Charles, *War in a Stringbag* (Leo Cooper, 1987)
3. Payne, Donald, *From the Cockpit No 10: Swordfish* (Ad Hoc Publications, 2008)
4. Payne, Donald, *op cit*.
5. Brand, Stanley, *Achtung! Swordfish! Merchant Aircraft Carriers* (Propagator Press, 2005)
6. Forty, George, *The Battle for Malta* (Ian Allan, 2003)
7. Lamb, Charles, *op cit*.
8. Payne, Donald, *op cit*.
9. Ott, Frank, *Air Power at Sea in the Second World War* (Society of Friends, Fleet Air Arm Museum, 2005)
10. Payne, Donald, *op cit*.
11. Sturtivant, Ray, *The Swordfish Story* (Cassell, 2000)

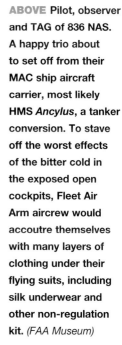

ABOVE Pilot, observer and TAG of 836 NAS. A happy trio about to set off from their MAC ship aircraft carrier, most likely HMS *Ancylus*, a tanker conversion. To stave off the worst effects of the bitter cold in the exposed open cockpits, Fleet Air Arm aircrew would accoutre themselves with many layers of clothing under their flying suits, including silk underwear and other non-regulation kit. *(FAA Museum)*

LEFT LS326, the grand old lady of the RN Historic Flight, 71 years young and still going strong – testimony to the dedication, perseverance and skills of her extensive band of supporters and the members of the Flight itself. *(RNHF)*

Chapter Eight

The engineer's view

Old fashioned she may be, but once one gets used to the biplane configuration and the neat common sense disposition of engine, fuel tanks and aircrew accommodation, checks and maintenance tasks prove to be logical and straightforward. Simplicity is the key characteristic when comparing the Swordfish with other warplanes of her generation and later.

OPPOSITE LS326 undergoing winter overhaul on the Flight.
(Jonathan Falconer)

Maintenance and repair

The following information is relevant for the Royal Navy Historic Flight Swordfish but is likely to vary from that which was applicable when the type was in service before, during and after the Second World War. The Royal Navy Historic Flight's three Swordfish are entered on the Military Register and as such they are subject to the airworthiness regulations laid down by the Military Aviation Authority (MAA). These are the same as those applicable to the Eurofighter Typhoon.

As with all other military aircraft the Swordfish has its own aircraft document set together with a series of type-specific maintenance manuals.

Maintenance of airframe, engine and all other elements is a cyclical affair. The safety of the aircraft and its personnel dictates that the frequency of this cycle is directly related (on a pro rata basis) to the number of flying hours undertaken.

LS326 AND W5856

These two aircraft are the airworthy examples operated by the Royal Navy Historic Flight. Being irreplaceable historic machines, each is limited to 50 flying hours per year. This 50 hours' flying time will principally be expended during the air display season, which extends from 1 April to 31 October.

In addition to the general constraint posed by the flying time limit, engine refurbishment will be required after 200 flying hours. Typically, therefore, this will take place at the end of every fourth year of operation. However, the need for refurbishment and/or replacement of other components or equipment occurs on the following basis:

BELOW LS326 and W5856 during winter overhauls. The port mainplane assembly has been detached from the fuselage. Being able to detach wings for repair and maintenance purposes is one benefit that stems from a wing-folding configuration. *(RNHF)*

- *Flying controls*   every 18 years.
- *Flexible pipelines for fuel and oil systems*
                        every 5–10 years
                        depending on wear, due
                        to variations in pressures.
- *Magnetos*   every 250 hours.
- *Fire extinguishers* every 10 years.
- *Parachutes*   every year.
- *First-aid kit*   every year.

The maintenance and servicing cycle

During the flying season, from April to October, servicing takes place on a daily basis while the aircraft is going to be airborne for display, on positioning flights or for air tests. Replenishment of fuel oil and air takes place as required, prior to flights and between them, when the aircraft is operating to a display schedule, as do checks of tyre pressures.

There is a clear division of responsibility regarding routine inspections and checks between maintainers working to the strict requirements of maintenance schedules, and the display or test pilot and his own pre-flight checks.

In addition, on flying display days the aircraft are inspected and serviced a) before flights; b) between flights (at the turnaround stage); and c) after completion of the day's flying.

INSPECTIONS

Typically the aircraft will be inspected and checked for the following states:

- Engine and fuel supply elements.
- The airframe itself. Examined externally.
- All movable control surfaces.
- Brake system pressures.
- Cockpit area safety equipment.
- Foreign object detection, confirming the absence of loose objects in the cockpit area and other inspectable parts.

Servicing tasks

After every 10 hours flying time:

- Spark plugs cleaned and/or replaced (x18).
- Oil samples taken and analysed.
- Oil filters cleaned.
- Reverse tyres

ABOVE LS326 trestled for major overhaul in March 2014, with the engine removed and cowling panels detached to allow access to components ahead of the firewall bulkhead and fuel tank area. The undercarriage legs have also been removed for NDT prior to the start of the 2014 air show season. *(Jonathan Falconer)*

BELOW Wheel and brake components, together with the oleo legs from the undercarriage set aside for examination. *(Jonathan Falconer)*

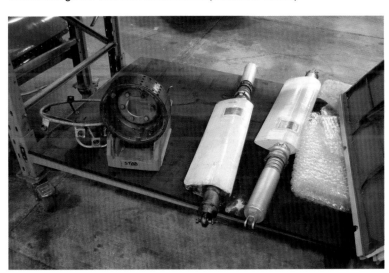

After every 25 hours' flying time:

- Flying controls, hinges and attachments inspected and lubricated.
- Check engine cylinder bolt tightness.
- Cylinder valve adjustment as necessary.
- Check fuel system and supply lines for possible leaks.
- Brakes and wheels – check for wear to linings and wheel bearings.
- Check fuel sample from carburettor for possible contamination.
- All detachable panels removed. Visual checks of framing and joints. Corrosion check.

Corrosion

A wide range of non-invasive techniques are available that will detect corrosion in its early stages. These include traditional X-ray methods, ultrasonic and eddy-current crack detection. Defects of the kind that will be picked up from these kinds of inspection divide principally into two categories, localised corrosion and cracking.

Localised corrosion may occur on the surface of framing or components and therefore will be readily identifiable. Some corrosion may develop internally, which is where one or other of the above suite of techniques will come into play.

A good example of hidden corrosion, to which the Swordfish structure is particularly susceptible, is that which develops inside the double-lobed upper and lower flanges of the wing spars. These elements are formed with a double-skin of rolled metal. The interstices of each flange can act as a moisture trap which, because they are hidden from view, require X-ray testing to identify the presence of corrosion.

Repair and replacement

An important characteristic of the Swordfish aircraft, reflecting the design philosophy of its makers, is that very little welding is used in the airframe and there is a minimum of bolted parts. Joints are connected using riveted fishplates.

The steel and alloy rivets used in construction are of a special conical type. Instead of having their heads turned over in the normal way they are expanded at the free end using a conical punch. Special tools are needed to remove and replace these rivets.

Steel parts have received anti-corrosion treatment in the form of cadmium plating. Alloy components receive anodic treatment. These parts, including tubing elements, are then given a coating of tung oil varnish. In an undisturbed state this registers the fact that the anti-corrosion treatment underneath is intact. Repairs and replacements must take account of these characteristics of manufacture.

Care must be taken when replacing any sections of fuselage frame tubing. Ends can be flattened for purposes of connection by using special blocks held in a vice. The flattened ends must be in the same angular plane.

The decision to repair or replace must take into account the work entailed in removing the damaged component and the difficulties involved in inserting a new one. However, repair may itself present its challenges. As an example, damaged mainplane and tail spars require the use of a very specific repair technique to restore their integrity.

In addition to cadmium plating treatment, the insides of wing and tailplane spars are given a soaking of boiled linseed oil. Surplus oil is thoroughly drained off before plugs are inserted.

Air Publication AP1517 gives four categories of repair:

- Negligible damage.
- Damage repairable by patching.
- Damage repairable by sleeving.
- Damage necessitating replacement.

BELOW **W5856 in the course of restoration by BAE Systems at Brough. Note the presence of an aircraft of much later vintage in the background!** *(BAE Systems)*

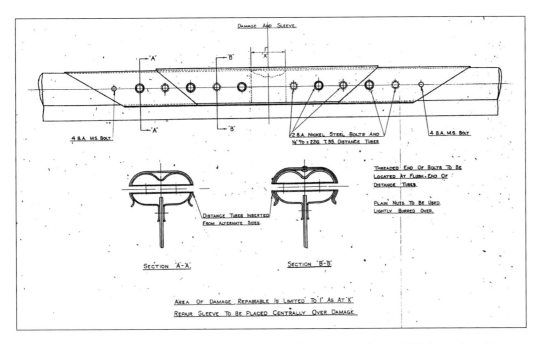

Fuselage strut and longeron repairs and replacements, including those applicable to the tail wedge are specified in AP1517 by individual members.

Wings

Reinforcing plates and spar boom repair sleeves are used to mend cracked or perforated spar webs or booms (ie flanges) respectively. The former will be secured with rivets and the latter will utilise nickel steel bolts secured with plain nuts.

No rib damage can be regarded as negligible, by reason of a rib's contribution as a component to the overall structural integrity. For this reason Standard Insertion Pieces are used in repairs and these are riveted across the damaged area of the rib.

Fabric repairs

The benefits that accrue from fabric covering on older aircraft designs are well recognised. Damage to an aircraft's metal skin either by gunfire or shipboard accident presented considerable problems when sustained far from land. Conversely repairs to the fabric covering of fuselage, mainplane or empennage were relatively simple and could be carried out at sea without much difficulty, even in poor weather conditions.

There are two levels of fabric repair. In the case of the minor task an insertion patch is trimmed and stitched to fit into the damaged area.

The damaged area is first cut out to an appropriate rectangular shape. All dope is cleaned from the edges of the damaged area. Then each of the four sides of the new hole is folded back underneath by ½in by making diagonal cuts in each of the four corners. This seam is then stitched. All cutting must respect the warp and weft of the fabric (ie it must be parallel or at right angles to the weave). A patch the exact size of the hole is inserted, held by

BELOW Port upper mainplane ready for covering. Note the Warren Girder form of the transverse wing ribs. *(Hornet Aviation)*

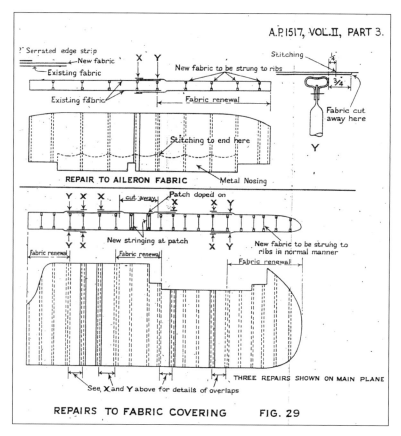

REPAIR TO AILERON FABRIC

REPAIRS TO FABRIC COVERING — FIG. 29

ABOVE The recommended technique shown in Air Ministry Repair Manual for the repair of fabric covering to wings and ailerons. (RNHF)

BELOW WRNS groundcrew at work servicing a Swordfish at a Royal Navy shore establishment. Some 75,000 WRNS were in service by 1944 undertaking a wide range of duties including servicing aircraft and acting as drivers, wireless mechanics and telephonists. (FAA Museum)

tacking and then stitched on to the hole sides, using a herringbone stitch. The whole repair at this stage must be firm and taut without creases or stress. Two coats of red dope applied in succession are brushed into the insertion patch with the first allowed to dry out before the second application. Finally a pre-cut serrated edged patch, 1in wider all round than the seam of the original, is doped on and given the appropriate final finish.

Wartime experiences of FAA ground crew

It was with comparative ease that the aircraft could be maintained and repaired up to certain limits. Under operational conditions the pilot played a key role in the identification of actual or developing defects. On landing, any irregularities, particularly in respect to the engine, would be reported straightaway to the groundcrew chief.

When embarked, the 30hr inspection was the most intensive one in the cycle. The 120hr inspection could normally only be undertaken when the ship was in harbour or the aircraft had been flown off to the RNAS.

So far as the division of labour was concerned, Swordfish and other FAA aircraft types were serviced by two mechanics (or artificers in naval terminology). These reflected the traditional division of responsibilities of rigger and fitter – or airframe and engine respectively.

In Atlantic and Arctic conditions it was inevitable that there would be high attrition rates on landing, with decks plunging through 20 to 30ft on occasion and some 14,000 tons of ship rising to meet the not over-strong Swordfish undercarriage as it hit the flight deck. That and such problems of swing in a cross-wind could produce spectacular accidents.

It says much for the simplicity of construction of the Swordfish, coupled with the dedication and imagination of its groundcrew, that there were instances of cannibalisation and rebuild after severe damage was sustained in such an accident.

In one such rebuild that took place aboard a MAC ship, no protective shelter was available since it was the tanker version and was thus devoid of hangar space. The rebuild process took place wholly in the open on the flight deck. On this occasion reusable fuselage and engine components were gathered together from three aircraft. These were combined with spares from the carrier's stock and united to create a flyable aircraft using makeshift lifting gear formed by the ship's mainmast and an ack-ack gun mounting. The first flight encountered some frightening moments due possibly to problems with trim, which were especially acute for the observer. In the end it was successful and the aircraft was able to land on again safely.

Unflyable aircraft did not stay long on the flight deck, or indeed in the small hangars of the MAC ships. Unless capable of repair while at sea, once cannibalised for all usable parts the remains of the airframe or a damaged engine would be tipped over the side. If adjudged repairable on shore, the damaged Swordfish might be lashed on deck in a position least detrimental to flying operations until the carrier reached port.

Eventually, when convoys were able to boast the luxury of two MAC ships, each was able to aid the other by the transfer at sea of equipment, spares and/or cannibalised items. In such situations aircraft serviceability rates could be expected to increase.

As with all military aircraft the Swordfish came with certain critical removable items. One such was what could be called the 'starting handle'. This was normally stowed in the rear cockpit on the starboard side. It is on record that on more than one occasion this critical item 'went missing'. If required for a test flight on land such a mishap would be quite easily and quickly resolved. But when at sea and commanded to start up in a ranged group of aircraft, if an observer had mislaid such an important piece of equipment it could lead to a delay in flying operations and would undoubtedly bring down the wrath of those on high.

Such a mishap raises the question of division of responsibility. The pilot and his two groundcrew worked as a team so in that sense ensuring the handle was available would be shared. However, the contents of the aircraft were the responsibility of the pilot as was ensuring the aircrew under him performed their duties efficiently.

ABOVE The undercarriage of this 816 NAS Swordfish collapsed after the pilot landed-on too heavily when the deck of HMS *Tracker* pitched violently while she was sailing in the North Atlantic. Note the crowd of men preparing to pull the aircraft clear. Note also the empty torpedo crutch beneath the fuselage and the RAF groundcrew sergeant disconnecting the electrical pigtail connectors from the R/Ps beneath the starboard wing. September/October 1943. *(IWM A19723)*

LEFT RAF and Royal Navy groundcrew refuel a Swordfish Mark III of 119 Squadron RAF Detachment at B65/Maldeghem, Belgium, 22 November 1944. Prominently visible in this head-on view is the Swordfish's Mark X ASV radar housed in the cumbersome-looking radome 'between the legs'. This attachment imposed further weight and drag penalties on an aircraft never known for its good turn of speed. *(IWM CL1638)*

REPLENISHMENT AND MAINTENANCE DETAILS

Engine fuel	AVGAS 100LL (main 155gal, aux 12½gal).
Engine oil	OMD 370 (alternative oil OMD 250).
Oleo struts	OM 15.
De-icing fluid	AL 11.
Compressor oil	OF300.
Tyre pressures	Main wheel 45psi, tail wheel 55psi.

Appendix 1

Swordfish survivors

Having been relegated to second-line duties such as target towing, the usual fate awaiting most British service aircraft at the end of their useful life was to be struck off charge before proceeding to the breaker's yard. Thus many famous types passed quietly into oblivion. However, there were certain exceptions whereby their lives might be prolonged. For instance, the tradition of installing retired airframes as gate guardians outside RAF, Royal Navy and Army Air Corps stations has ensured the survival of a select number of significant aircraft over the years. Several historic types continued in existence as Instructional Airframes. These were deposited as training equipment at military engineering colleges and apprentice schools.

Of more significance were the actions of a handful of enlightened manufacturers. Sensitive to the importance of the contribution their product had made to aviation heritage these firms intervened, setting aside examples of their work and thereby allowing them to escape the breaker's blowtorch. Fairey's were one such plane maker. That we still have a Fairey Fulmar, an early 1940s naval fighter of which only relatively small numbers were built, is due to the foresight of the firm and its owners led by the legendary Sir Richard Fairey. The prototype rests now in the Fleet Air Arm Museum, Yeovilton, as a fitting tribute to a doughty warrior that met German, Italian and Japanese attacks on British ships during the early years of the Second World War.

Bearing in mind this Fairey tradition it is no surprise, therefore, that their other more legendary design, the Swordfish, benefited from this kind of foresight. Sir Richard Fairey reputedly spotted a small number of the aircraft near the Fairey factory in a decaying state in the early 1950s and selected LS326 for restoration to flying condition. From 1955 onwards, initially registered as G-AJVH, this machine (a veteran of the Atlantic convoy MAC ships) has thrilled spectators at air shows and Royal Navy commemorative events. The aircraft's future was assured in 1960 when she was presented by Westland Aircraft to the Royal Navy, from whose ownership she has been passed to her present operators, the Royal Navy Historic Flight.

The Royal Navy Historic Flight is fortunate in possessing two other Swordfish, namely W5856 and NF389. Since these are respectively of the Mark I and Mark III types, taken together with LS326, a Mark II, their presence ensures the Flight has examples of all three marks.

RIGHT AND OPPOSITE Vintage Wings of Canada's Swordfish Mark IV, HS554/C-GEVS, airborne over the beautiful landscape of Gatineau, Quebec, on 21 September 2011, with pilot Bob Childerhose at the controls. *(Richard Mallory Allnutt/Vintage Wings of Canada)*

Swordfish Mark I, W5856
Royal Navy Historic Flight, RNAS Yeovilton, UK
Airworthy

Swordfish Mark II, HS618
Fleet Air Arm Museum, Yeovilton, UK
Static display

Swordfish Mark II, LS326
Royal Navy Historic Flight, RNAS Yeovilton, UK
Airworthy

Swordfish Mark II, 'NS122'
Canada Aviation and Space Museum, Ottawa, Canada
'NS122' is a fictitious serial. Original identity lost during aircraft's
storage outdoors on a farm in Tillsonburg, Ontario

Swordfish Mark III, NF370
Imperial War Museum, Duxford, UK
Static display

Swordfish Mark III, NF389
Royal Navy Historic Flight, RNAS Yeovilton, UK
Under restoration

Swordfish Mark IV, HS164
Ownership and location not known

Swordfish Mark IV, HS469
Shearwater Aviation Museum, Nova Scotia, Canada
Static display

Swordfish Mark IV, HS491
Malta Aviation Museum, Ta'Qali
Awaiting restoration

Swordfish Mark IV, HS498/HS509
Reynolds-Alberta Museum, Canada
Static display

Swordfish Mark IV, HS503
RAF Museum, Stafford, UK
Reserve collection

Swordfish Mark IV, HS554/C-GEVS
Vintage Wings of Canada, Gatineau, Quebec, Canada
Airworthy

W5856 is without doubt the oldest surviving example of its type in the world. Built like the other two by Blackburn, and therefore strictly speaking a 'Blackfish', she is known to have served in the Mediterranean theatre and had then been passed to the Royal Canadian Navy. Restored by BAE Systems in 1990 she was then given to the RN Historic Flight. Like LS326 she has survived threats to her continued survival and airworthiness through corrosion problems. That she has survived is principally due to the generosity of BAE Systems. They have lavished great skill in rebuilding wings and wing spars afflicted with metal corrosion.

Like some other British designs of the Second World War era, there is a strong Canadian dimension to the Swordfish story. Shipped to Canada in the early years of the war, from 1943 onwards around 100 of the type provided training aircraft under the British Commonwealth (originally Empire) Air Training Scheme. Principally used to train naval air gunners (or TAGs as the Royal Navy called them) at the Air Gunnery School in Yarmouth, Nova Scotia, Swordfish also served in the associated role of target drogue towers. Surprisingly some of the type went on to provide instructional aircraft for Royal Canadian Naval Reserve units after war's end with a handful surviving in flying condition until late 1946.

Eventually the majority of surviving Canadian Swordfish were scrapped. However, some half a dozen in various states of decay were sold off at auction with at least one airframe and engine finding its way back to the UK as a museum static display acquisition.

At least two Canadian survivors grace museums in Nova Scotia and at Ottawa. A third – C-GEVS, ex-HS554 – is airworthy and is flown by Vintage Wings of Canada.

There are additional static display examples in the Malta Aviation Museum and the Commemorative Air Force Museum in Texas with a replica in New Zealand (DK791).

Finally a Mark III version wearing RAF markings is to be seen at the Imperial War Museum's Duxford site in Cambridgeshire, and the FAA Museum at Yeovilton displays a Mark II as a static exhibit, but one which reflects parts of more than one aircraft.

Appendix 2

Glossary of abbreviations

AA (fire)   Ack-Ack. Abbreviation for anti-aircraft. Derived from the early phonetic alphabet.

A&AEE   Aeroplane and Armament Experimental Establishment. Centre for performance trials of military aircraft.

ADDL   Aerodrome Dummy Deck Landing. Provision on runways at Naval Air Stations for training purposes.

AP   Armour piercing.

ASI   Airspeed Indicator. Instrument in pilot's cockpit.

ASV   Air-to-Surface Vessel. Term applied to successive marks of aerial radar used for that purpose.

ATDU   Aircraft Torpedo Development Unit.

Biber   German two-man midget submarine, active in early 1945.

Cabane   The raised centre section of the upper mainplane, supported above the fuselage.

Capt   Captain (Royal Navy). Distinguishes rank rather than function.

Cdr   Commander

Cucumber   Codeword or nickname for aerial mine.

D/C   Depth charge.

DCLO   Deck Landing Control Officer, otherwise known as 'Bats'. Charged with guiding naval pilots to safe carrier deck landings.

DLT   Deck Landing Training.

DTD   Directorate of Technical Development. Important post in the Admiralty, influencing aspects of naval aviation.

FAA   Fleet Air Arm. Originated post-1918 when the RAF took over the responsibility for naval aviation. Retained when this returned to Admiralty control.

Flak   Short for *Fliegerabwehrkanone*, German anti-aircraft fire.

FPTU   Floatplane Training Unit. Tasked with conversion of pilots from landplane version of Swordfish.

Gardening   Codename for aerial mine-laying activity.

Gosport Tube   Simple device enabling aircrew to communicate between cockpits.

HE   High Explosive.

Lt   Lieutenant, naval rank.

Lt Cdr   Lieutenant Commander, next senior naval rank to lieutenant.

MAC ship   Merchant Aircraft Carrier. A temporary conversion of small tankers and grain ships by the addition of a flush flight deck.

MAEE   Marine Aircraft Experimental Establishment. Equivalent station for seaplane testing of A&AEE (see above).

m/g   Machine gun on Swordfish, one fixed, one movable.

NAS   Naval Air Squadron or pre-April 1914, Naval Air Service.

PO   Petty Officer, senior non-commissioned officer.

Radar   RAdio Direction And Range, replaced RDF (Radio Direction Finding).

RAE   Royal Aircraft Establishment.

RATOG   Rocket Assisted Take Off Gear.

R/P   Rocket projectile.

RPM   Revolutions per minute.

S/E   Special Equipment, a codename for radar.

TSR   Torpedo Spotter Reconnaissance.

VGO   Vickers Gas-Operated, type of light machine gun.

Index